Grenfell: System Failure
Scenes from the Inquiry

Richard Norton-Taylor

with Nicolas Kent

T0054204

methuen | drama

LONDON · NEW YORK · OXFORD · NEW DELHI · SYDNEY

METHUEN DRAMA
Bloomsbury Publishing Plc
50 Bedford Square, London, WC1B 3DP, UK
1385 Broadway, New York, NY 10018, USA
29 Earlsfort Terrace, Dublin 2, Ireland

BLOOMSBURY, METHUEN DRAMA and the Methuen
Drama logo are trademarks of Bloomsbury Publishing Plc

First published in Great Britain 2023

Cover design by Bob King Creative

A catalogue record for this book is available from the British Library.

Library of Congress Control Number: 2023931036

ISBN: PB: 978-1-3504-0150-1
ePDF: 978-1-3504-0152-5
eBook: 978-1-3504-0151-8

Series: Modern Plays

Typeset by Mark Heslington Ltd, Scarborough, North Yorkshire

To find out more about our authors and books visit
www.bloomsbury.com and sign up for our newsletters.

Grenfell: System Failure
Scenes from the Inquiry
by Richard Norton-Taylor with Nicolas Kent

The Inquiry

Chairman SIR MARTIN MOORE-BICK	Thomas Wheatley
Counsel to the Inquiry RICHARD MILLETT QC	Ron Cook
Assisted by KATE GRANGE QC	Sally Giles

Witnesses and lawyers in order of appearance:

HISAM CHOUCAIR	
(*Bereaved family member*)	Shahzad Ali
ADRIAN PARGETER	
(*Head of Technical and Marketing, Kingspan*)	Nicholas Chambers
DEBORAH FRENCH	
(*UK Sales Manager, Arconic*)	Madeleine Bowyer
Professor Leslie Thomas QC	
(*BSR Group Barrister*)	Derek Elroy
Andrew Roe	
(*Commissioner, London Fire Brigade*)	David Michaels
Imran Khan QC	
(*BSR Group Solicitor*)	Tanveer Ghani
Dr Sarah Colwell	
(*Building Research Establishment*)	Sophie Duval
Brian Martin	
(*Employed by the Building Research Establishment 1999–2008; Principal Construction Professional, Department of Communities and Local Government 2008–*)	Nigel Betts
Lord Pickles	
(*Secretary of State for Communities and Local Government 2010–2015*)	Howard Crossley
Nick Hurd	
(*Minister for Grenfell Victims 2017–*)	David Michaels
Understudy	David Boyle

Produced & Directed by	Nicolas Kent
Inquiry Room recreated by	Miki Jablkowska & Matt Eagland
Lighting Design by	Matt Eagland
Sound & Video Design by	Andy Graham
Costume Design by	Carly Brownbridge
Casting by	Amy Ball CDG
Assistant Director	Esme Sears
Community Liaison	Suresh Grover

For Smart Entertainment

Executive Producer	Peter Huntley
General Managers	Callum Runciman & Jack Sterne
General Management Associate	Lucy Rahim
Production Accountant	Martin Ball

Marketing	Jan Baister
Press & PR	Emma Holland & Didi Ralph for Emma Holland PR
Artwork	Bob King Creative
Photography	Beresford Hodge

Grenfell: System Failure – Scenes from the Inquiry was first performed at the Playground Theatre, London, in February 2023 and subsequently at The Tabernacle and the Marylebone Theatre, London, until March 2023.

Phase 1 of the Inquiry opened at Holborn in November 2017 and concluded in December 2018. Phase 2 of the Inquiry opened at Paddington in January 2019.

For some of the 2020 hearings, due to the Covid-19 pandemic, there was restricted public access to the Inquiry room, and later in the year hearings were conducted remotely by video link.

The Inquiry concluded in November 2022. The final report is expected in the latter part of 2023.

Running time: 2 hours and 20 minutes with a 15-minute interval.

PRODUCTION TEAM

Production / Stage Manager	Miki Jablkowska
Deputy Stage Manager	Olivia Haw
Technician & Sound Operator	Tom Codd
Production Carpenter	Dan Speight

CO-PRODUCERS

	The Playground Theatre
Co-Artistic Director	Anthony Biggs
Founder & Co-Artistic Director	Peter Tate
Outreach Director	Paul O'Mahony
General Manager	Helena Hipólito
Deputy General Manager & Marketing	Holly-Anne White
Technical Manager	Steven Dean Moore
Outreach Coordinator	Phil Correia
Outreach Facilitator	Talitha Wing
The Board	Sally Davies (Chair), Andrew Bailey, Anni Domingo, Naomi Tate and Amanda Waggott

Many people and organisations have generously given their time and help to make this production and we would like to gratefully acknowledge their contribution: Anthony Biggs, Jack Bradley, Bristol Costume Services, Nica Burns, Jon Catty, Lisa Forrell, Bob King, Belinda Lang, Mary Lauder, Laurence Miller, The National Theatre, Hilary Norrish, Paddington Arts for rehearsal facilities, Daniel Perillous, Lin Potter, Stage Sound Services, Peter Tate, Gillian Slovo and Susan Whiddington.

Websites and contacts for the following Grenfell organisations are:

The Grenfell Foundation | www.grenfellfoundation.org.uk

Grenfell United | www.grenfellunited.org.uk

Justice4Grenfell | www.justice4grenfell.org

Lancaster West | www.lancwest.com

Next of Kin | grenfellnextofkin@gmail.com

SMART ENTERTAINMENT MANAGEMENT

Smart Entertainment provides general management, executive producing, accountancy and consultancy services for the theatre and live entertainment sector. Its team have worked on over 125 productions. Smart's recent clients include Nick of Time Productions (*Grenfell: Value Engineering*), Hartshorn – Hook Enterprises (including *Peaky Blinders: The Rise*, *Doctor Who: Time Fracture*, *Amélie* and *The Great Gatsby*), the London Musical Theatre Orchestra (including *A Christmas Carol* at the Dominion, 2020), Oxford Playhouse, and Northampton Royal & Derngate. www.smartentertainment.co

NICK OF TIME PRODUCTIONS

Nick of Time Productions Ltd was founded in 2012. Productions produced include *The Nightmares of Carlos Fuentes* by Rashid Razaq at the Arcola Theatre and Mark Thomas' *Check-up: Our NHS@70* (Fringe First winner) at the Traverse Theatre, The Arcola, Battersea Arts Centre, The Other Palace as well as a national tour. In 2022 it co-produced *Playboy of the West Indies* – the musical by Mustapha Matura, Clement Ishmael, Dominique LeGendre and Nicolas Kent at the Birmingham Rep.

THE PLAYGROUND THEATRE

The Playground Theatre is a multi-disciplinary performing arts incubator and venue in W10. By fostering a supportive environment for open-ended experimentation, The Playground serves as a haven for emerging and established artists alike to come and play – to exercise the essential creative muscles that spark authentic, innovative works. As a registered charity, The Playground also delivers outreach programmes, and mental health initiatives that strengthen the resilience of the local community through creative engagement. www.theplaygroundtheatre.london

THE TABERNACLE

Located in the heart of Notting Hill, The Tabernacle is a Grade II-listed building boasting a beautiful, curved Romanesque façade of red brick and terracotta, and towers with broach spires on either side. With a variety of spaces on offer including the Theatre, Gallery, Dance Studio, Meeting Room and Garden, there's always something going on at The Tabernacle. Open from 9:00am daily it hosts live music, theatre, exhibitions and regular activities.

MARYLEBONE THEATRE

Marylebone Theatre is a new cross-arts venue in London, which presents the best new writing alongside high-quality dance, music and spoken word, carving out a special place on the London cultural scene as a beautiful and grand but intimate setting. The theatre supports local groups through its funded community-in-the-arts scheme and runs a youth theatre and arts-based educational programme.

PADDINGTON ARTS (Rehearsal Facilities)

Paddington Arts is a Youth Arts organisation committed to developing talent and creativity in the community. Paddington Arts work with a number of local community groups, dance, film, television and theatre companies and a variety of cultural and arts organisations.

Nick of Time Productions and the Playground Theatre gratefully acknowledge the generous financial support for this production and the SYSTEMS Education Programme from the following charitable foundations:

and the substantial financial support from the following organisations and people:

Mary Clancy, Doughty Street Chambers, John Lyon's Charity, The Mercers' Company, Peter Wilson and the John S. Cohen Foundation.

The production is not-for-profit and is not funded by Arts Council England.

Shahzad Ali

Theatre credits include: *False Accounts: Exposing the Post Office Cover-Up* (Questors).

Nigel Betts

Theatre credits include: *The Good Life* (UK Tour); *Steel* (Sheffield Theatres); *Albion* (Almeida); *Wonderland* (Hampstead); *Pastoral* (Soho); *Three Days in the Country*, *One Man Two Guv'nors* and *War Horse* (National Theatre and Theatre Royal Haymarket/Gillian Lynne); *Aladdin* (Lyric Hammersmith); *The 39 Steps* (Criterion); *Up 'n' Under* (Playhouse); *Henry IV* (Wyndham's); *As You Like It* (Old Vic); *Tinderbox* (Bush); *The Constant Couple* and *The Recruiting Officer* (Blue Eagle); *A New Way to Please You*, *Sejanus: His Fall*, *Thomas More* and *Night of the Soul* (RSC); *Eden End* and *Macbeth* (West Yorkshire Playhouse) and *Neville's Island* (Watford Palace).

Madeleine Bowyer

Theatre credits include: *Pygmalion* (Japan and International tour); *Moby Dick* (Walk The Plank); *Bromley, Bedlam, Bethlehem* (Old Red Lion); *The Great Gatsby* (Wilton's Music Hall); *Breakfast Soldiers* (Manchester Contact); *Our Day Out* (Sheffield Crucible); *Death and the Ploughman* (Gate); and *Execution of Justice* (Southwark Playhouse).

David Boyle

Theatre credits include: *Best of Enemies* (Noël Coward); *The Mousetrap* (St Martin's); *Fawlty Towers Gourmet Cabaret* (UK Tour and Edinburgh Festival); *Jeff Wayne's The War of the Worlds: Immersive Experience* (dotdotdot); *Jack and the Beanstalk* (Millfield Arts); *Jeepers Creepers* (Leicester Square); *The Phantom Raspberry Blower of Old Town* (The Other Palace); *Being Sellers* (and Off-Broadway) and *The Actors Market* (Waterloo East); *Newley – The Fool Who Dared to Dream* (Upstairs at The Gatehouse) and *Newley – The Singer and His Songs* (The Actors Centre and Edinburgh Festival).

Nicholas Chambers

Theatre credits include: *The Department of Distractions* and *Life and Loves of a Nobody* (Third Angel); *Hamlet's Playground* (CREW); *The*

Incredible Doctor Guttman (UK Tour); *The Great Gatsby* (Wilton's Music Hall); *My Dad's a Birdman* (Sheffield Crucible); and *Air Guitar* (Bristol Old Vic).

Ron Cook

Theatre credits include: *Grenfell: Value Engineering* (Tabernacle, Birmingham Rep and Channel 4); *Girl from the North Country* (Old Vic); *The Children* (Broadway); *Our Country's Good, The Recruiting Officer* and *Cloud Nine* (Royal Court); *Europe, Faith Healer, Trelawny of the Wells, Richard II, King Lear, Juno & the Paycock* and *Glengarry Glen Ross* (Donmar Warehouse); *The Homecoming, Henry V* and *Hamlet* (Broadway); *The Ruling Class* (Trafalgar Studios); *Twelfth Night* and *Art* (Wyndham's); and *The Seafarer, Howard Katz, Black* and *Snow* (National Theatre).

Howard Crossley

Theatre credits include: *Hamlet, A Midsummer Night's Dream, Coriolanus, Two Gentleman of Verona, Julius Caesar, Pentecost, Camino Real, Romeo & Juliet, A Woman Killed With Kindness, The Virtuoso* and *The Merry Wives of Windsor* (RSC); *A Midsummer Night's Dream* (RSC on Broadway); *As You Like It* and *Enemy of the People* (Aquila, New York); *Henry IV* (Wyndham's); *Billy Elliot* (Victoria Palace); and *The Lion King* (Lyceum).

Sophie Duval

Theatre credits include: *The Watsons* (Chichester Festival and Menier Chocolate Factory); *The Crucible* (The Yard); *The Curious Incident of the Dog In the Night-Time* (National Theatre); *Great Expectations* (RSC); *Anne Boleyn, All's Well That Ends Well, Bedlam, As You Like It* and *A New World* (Shakespeare's Globe); *Unless* and *Soap* (Stephen Joseph, Scarborough); *Americans* (Oxford Stage Company); *Great Expectations* (Bristol Old Vic); *Humble Boy* (Gielgud); *Anne and Zef, House/Garden, The Rivals* (Salisbury Playhouse); and *A Christmas Carol* (Lyric Hammersmith).

Derek Elroy

Theatre credits include: *Christmas in the Sunshine* (Unicorn); *The Playboy of the West Indies* (Birmingham Rep); *Jack and the Beanstalk* (Orchard, Dartford); *Grenfell: Value Engineering* (Tabernacle, Birmingham Rep and Channel 4); *Grimm Tales* (Dukes, Lancaster);

Aladdin (Churchill); *Calendar Girls* (UK Tour); *Screwed* (Theatre 503); *The Wind in the Willows* (Rose Theatre Kingston); *One Man, Two Guvnors* (National Theatre, Adelphi and UK Tour); *The Harder They Come* (Playhouse); *The Blues Brothers* (European Tour) and *Foe* (Complicité).

Tanveer Ghani

Theatre credits include: *Drawing the Line* and *Loose Ends* (Hampstead); *In The Balance* (The New End); *Macbeth* (Tricycle); and *Dusky Warriors* (Theatre Royal Stratford East).

Sally Giles

Theatre credits include: *Grenfell: Value Engineering* (Tabernacle, Birmingham Rep and Channel 4); *The Colour of Justice* (Tricycle and UK Tour), *Bloody Sunday* and *Justifying War* (Tricycle); *Sweet Bird of Youth* (National Theatre); *As You Like It* (Southwark Playhouse), *Things We Do for Love* (Scarborough); *Women Laughing* (Watford Playhouse); and *For Services Rendered* (Salisbury).

David Michaels

Theatre credits include: *Grenfell: Value Engineering* (The Tabernacle, Birmingham Rep and Channel 4); *Curious Incident of the Dog in the Night-Time* (UK and International tour); *Ticking* (Trafalgar Studios); *The 39 Steps* (UK Tour); *A Doll's House* (Coventry); *Herding Cats* (Hampstead); *Death and the Maiden* (Salisbury); *Betrayal* (Peter Hall Company); *Three Sisters* (Birmingham Rep); *The Changing Room* (Duke of York's); *Fuente Ovejuna* (National Theatre); *A Taste of Honey* (Nottingham); and *The Hutton Inquiry*, *Called to Account* and *The War Next Door* (Tricycle).

Thomas Wheatley

Theatre credits include: *Grenfell: Value Engineering* (Tabernacle, Birmingham Rep and Channel 4); *Chilcot* (Lowry); *Half the Picture*, *Nuremberg*, *Srebrenica*, *The Colour of Justice*, *Justifying War*, *Bloody Sunday*, *Called to Account* and *Tactical Questioning* (Tricycle).

Richard Norton-Taylor

Former defence and security editor of the *Guardian*.

Journalist and playwright, contributor to the website, Declassified UK. Books include: *Truth is a Difficult Concept* and *The State of Secrecy*. Winner of two Freedom of Information Campaigns awards and Liberty's Human Rights Campaign award. Collaborated with Nicolas Kent on eight verbatim plays including *The Colour of Justice*, *Bloody Sunday* and *Justifying War*. His theatre work has been published and broadcast on the BBC. It won an Olivier Award in 2005.

Nicolas Kent

Director: Tricycle Theatre (1984–2012).

Productions included: *Half the Picture*, *The Stephen Lawrence Inquiry*, *Nuremberg*, *Srebrenica* and *Bloody Sunday* (Olivier Award), all broadcast by the BBC. Also *Guantanamo* (Olivier nomination), *The Riots* and the trilogy: *The Great Game – Afghanistan* (Olivier nomination; London/New York/Washington).

At the National Theatre: *Another World* and *All the President's Men* (co-production National Theatre/Public Theater).

He has directed for TV and at the RSC, the Royal Court, Donmar, Young Vic, Hampstead, in the West End and in America. Most recently: *Grenfell: Value Engineering* at the Tabernacle and for Channel 4 and co-directed *Playboy of the West Indies – the Musical* at the Birmingham Rep.

Miki Jablkowska

Miki has worked principally in automation on West End musicals. Stage credits include: *Miss Saigon*, *Sunset Boulevard*, *Spamalot*, *Ghost*, *Jersey Boys* and *Les Misérables* (Paris). She has also worked on numerous productions at the Royal Opera House.

Miki would like to thank both Nicolas Kent on this truly important production, and artist Emily Fuller, who has worked with Grenfell survivors on mosaic art which commemorates the tragedy.

Matt Eagland

Matthew trained at Guildhall, and was head of the lighting department at Guildford, and then Cambridge Arts Theatre during the 1990s. He has subsequently designed the lighting for many productions and events throughout the UK and around the world.

Highlights include: *The Children* (Salisbury Playhouse); *The Playboy of the West Indies* (Birmingham Rep); *The Nightmares of Carlos Fuentes* (Arcola); *This Was a Man* (Finborough); *Flow and Ignis* (Print Room); *Derren Brown's Svengali* (Shaftesbury); and *Broken Glass* (Vaudeville).

Andy Graham

Sound Design/Composition credits include: *The Chalk Garden*, *The Shawshank Redemption* and *Dial M for Murder* (Theatre Royal Windsor); *Grenfell: Value Engineering* (The Tabernacle, Birmingham Rep & Channel 4); *The Upstart Crow* (Gielgud); *The Book Thief*, *One Man, Two Guvnors*, *Beryl*, *Seagulls* and *Treasure Island* (Octagon, Bolton); *The Last Temptation Of Boris Johnson* (Park); *The Season* (Theatre Royal, Northampton); *Jess And Joe Forever* and *Alice In Wonderland* (Stephen Joseph); *The Greatest Wealth*, *One Hand Tied Behind Us* and *Monstrous Tales* (The Old Vic); *The Hound of the Baskervilles* (English Theatre Frankfurt); *Aladdin* (Lyric, Hammersmith); *FUP* (Kneehigh); *Lizzie Siddal* and *The Nightmares Of Carlos Fuentes* (Arcola).

Carly Brownbridge

Carly is a set, costume and video designer. She has an MA in Theatre Design from Bristol Old Vic Theatre School. She won the John Elvery Prize for Theatre Design 2020.

Stage credits include: *The Parent Show* (Theatre Royal Plymouth), *Telethon* (Touring), *Snow White* (Theatre503), *Grenfell: Value Engineering* (Tabernacle Theatre / Birmingham Rep), *A Right Royal Rumpus* (Eastbourne Theatres), *Red Light Winter* (Turbine Theatre), *La Traviata* (Festival Eva Ganizate), *If Not Now, When?* (Touring), *North of Providence + Dolores* (Site Specific Live Broadcast), *The Laramie Project* (Bristol Old Vic), *Cece's Speakeasy* (The Albany), *The Wind Blows Free* (Tristan Bates Theatre).

Esme Sears

Esme trained at Drama Studio London.

Acting credits include: *Gaze* (Northern Stage); *Much Ado About Nothing* (1623 Shakespeare Theatre Company); *The Wizard of Oz* (Leeds Playhouse); *The Jungle Book* (Derby Theatre); *Return of the Soldier* (Hope Mill & New Wolsey Theatres); *A Little Night Music* (Storyhouse Theatre); *The Crucible* (Storyhouse Theatre); *Parade* (Frogmore Mill); *Cinderella* (Derby Theatre) and *State of Fear: Britain For Breakfast* (Southwark Playhouse).

Narrator for RNIB Talking books; audiobooks include *Stranded* by Sarah Goodwin, *Arctic Zoo* by Robert Muchamore, *Ellie and the Cat* by Malorie Blackman.

Director credits include: *Do You Get Your Hair Permed?* (Wolverhampton Arena Theatre).

According to the latest published figures, the Inquiry has cost £130m, including more than £60m on lawyers. Kensington and Chelsea Borough spent more than £400m on recovery measures after the fire including rehousing survivors and consultants' fees. More than fifty law firms were involved and more than ten QCs (now KCs). Arconic, the firm that made the combustible cladding panels, has reportedly spent more than £50m on consultants and lawyers.

The Inquiry has disclosed more than 320,000 documents. More than 180 police officers and civilian staff were assigned to the investigation, well in excess of 31 million documents had been gathered, 2,500 physical exhibits had been seized, 2,332 witness statements had been taken from 1,144 witnesses, and 383 companies had been identified as having some involvement in or connection to the construction or refurbishment of Grenfell Tower. There were 642 core participants, including the bereaved, survivors and residents of the tower, trade unions, commercial organisations and public bodies deemed to have a 'significant interest' in matters raised during the Inquiry. Victims and their families received funding for their legal representation.

The Grenfell Tower Inquiry was established under the 2005 Inquiries Act, giving the chairman, former appeal court judge Sir Martin Moore-Bick, the power to compel the production of documents and summon witnesses to give evidence on oath. The Attorney-General, Suella Braverman, agreed to demands some two years after the start of the Inquiry, by the companies' lawyers – who were increasingly concerned about evidence accumulating against their clients – that their witnesses would not be prosecuted as a result of evidence they gave to the Inquiry. They had warned the chairman that witnesses might withhold evidence and could speak openly only if the attorney gave an undertaking that they would be protected from self-incrimination, as had been granted to witnesses at previous public inquiries, including the Saville Inquiry into the Bloody Sunday shooting of unarmed civil rights marchers in Derry.

Such protection applies only to evidence individual witnesses gave in answers to questions, not to evidence contained in emails or other documents. The attorney's undertaking does not prevent criminal prosecutions arising from a separate investigation by the Metropolitan Police.

The Inquiry was shown a transcript of a telephone conversation which explicitly raised the question of criminal charges. The transcript recorded John Simmons of Simco, an installation firm, telling Deborah French, Arconic's former UK sales manager, that the company may be 'guilty of corporate manslaughter' because it had not revealed the true performance of its panels and that tests on the materials found it 'goes up like a fucking bonfire'. Lawyers representing survivors and the bereaved suggested charges of 'gross negligence manslaughter' were a possible outcome of the police investigation.

More than 800 bereaved and survivors from Grenfell Tower and over 100 firefighters are seeking up to tens of millions of pounds in the High Court in compensation from companies and organisations involved in Grenfell Tower's refurbishment.

The Inquiry's terms of reference included the cause of the fire, decisions surrounding its refurbishment, the adequacy of building regulations, and the response of the London Fire Brigade, Kensington and Chelsea borough council and the government.

Timeline:

14 June 2017, the fire

15 June 2017, Prime Minister Theresa May announced a public inquiry

28 June 2017, Sir Martin Moore-Bick appointed to chair the Inquiry

September 2017, the Inquiry's first hearing

June 2018, Phase 1 begins, focusing on the fire, how it spread and the response to it

December 2018, conclusion of Phase 1

October 2019, Moore-Bick publishes his Phase 1 report

January 2020, start of Phase 2 hearings which examined how and why the fire spread

February 2020, Attorney General agreed to protect witnesses from self-incrimination after their lawyers warned that they might refuse to answer questions without such an assurance

March 2020, Covid outbreak leads to suspension of inquiry

July 2020, resumption of inquiry with limited attendance and some witnesses appearing by video link

November 2020, decision to give some evidence by video link

December 2020, inquiry suspended due to positive Covid test

February 2021 evidence resumes with video evidence

April 2021, limited attendance hearings resume September 2021, the Inquiry re-opens to the public

10 November 2022, conclusion of Phase 2 hearings

The Inquiry's final report is expected to be published by the end of 2023

The Inquiry was divided into seven Modules addressing: an overview of the cladding, the cladding products and their testing, complaints and communications with the residents and fire safety orders, firefighting, the role of government, further evidence from expert witnesses, and the aftermath of the fire.

With the exception of a very few phrases, denoted by square brackets and added only to clarify points of fact, the words are those exchanged between the witnesses and those questioning them.

The four volumes of Phase 1 of the chairman's report and the Executive Summary for Phase 1 of the report may be found on the Grenfell Tower Inquiry website:

www.grenfelltowerinquiry.org.uk

Grenfell: System Failure

Scenes from the Inquiry

Glossary

ACM: Aluminium Composite Material rainscreen cladding panels made of highly flammable polyethylene (PE) plastic cores sandwiched between thin aluminium sheets. Manufactured by the French subsidiary of a US company, Arconic. Cheaper than fire-retardant alternatives, the Inquiry revealed it had failed fire safety tests. Cited by Moore-Bick as the principal reason why the flames spread so rapidly up, down and around Grenfell Tower. Banned by the British government in November 2018, more than a year after the fire.

Approved Document B: Referred to as 'the bible for the construction industry', it sets fire safety standards for buildings. In 2020, the government revised the document saying sprinklers should be provided in individual flats, and high-rise buildings must have much clearer signs for firefighters.

BBA: The British Board of Agrément, the inspection authority which issues certificates and is responsible for maintaining high standards of quality and safety in building materials and construction. It wrongly certified the ACM panels and Arconic withheld crucial fire test information.

BRE: The Building Research Establishment. It was privatised in 1997 and became dependent on commercial clients; it was embroiled in allegations, strongly denied, that it advised Celotex, the manufacturer of RS5000 insulation panels surrounding Grenfell Tower, to help it get round fire tests.

BSR: Bereaved, Survivors and Residents of Grenfell Tower.

FSG: Fire Survival Guidance to give to callers to the Fire Brigade trapped as a result of a fire. It is defined as the advice and guidance given by fire control personnel to people at risk, who are directly affected by fire, heat or smoke and cannot get to a place of safety.

FSG would follow the three principles of emergency call handling – 'assess, protect, assist rescue'.

KALC: Kensington Academy and Leisure Centre, designed by Studio E.

KCTMO: The Royal Borough of Kensington and Chelsea (RBKC)'s Tenants Management Association, set up in 1996 to operate at arm's length from the Borough to manage housing. It commissioned the refurbishment of Grenfell Tower and was a main player in the cost-cutting exercise. Also referred to as the *TMO*.

PIR: Polyisocyanurate (foam core insulation). A combustible product.

Rainscreen: A system made with a bearing wall, an insulation layer, and a cladding material that is fixed to the building using a supporting structure providing an air cavity designed to allow continuous ventilation.

RS5000: The main exterior insulation panels, made by Celotex, with flammable PIR (polyisocyanurate), which burns when exposed to heat and gives off toxic cyanide fumes. RS5000 was a rebranded FR5000 panel that had earlier failed fire safety tests. The company covered up tests on RS5000 that were fixed. K15 flammable insultation panels, made by an Irish company, Kingspan, were also used on Grenfell Tower and also failed fire tests that were covered up.

Stay-Put Policy: Fire Brigade advice based on the assumption that a fire would be contained in a building through 'compartmentation'. Residents were advised to stay put 'unless the fire is in or affecting your flat'.

Value Engineering: The term traditionally has meant the process of achieving the best and most efficient value for money with the most suitable and practical materials. In the context of Grenfell Tower and its refurbishment it became a euphemism for cost-cutting at the expense of safety.

Characters

Witnesses and Lawyers for BSR Groups

Hisam Choucair
Adrian Pargeter
Deborah French
Leslie Thomas QC
Andy Roe
Imran Khan QC
Sarah Colwell
Brian Martin
Lord Pickles
Nick Hurd

Legal Team

Sir Martin Moore-Bick, *Chairman of the Inquiry*
Richard Millett QC, *Lead counsel to the Inquiry*
Kate Grange QC, *Deputy lead counsel to the Inquiry*

Slide: 'From the evidence of:
HISAM CHOUCAIR [who lost six members of his family in the fire – his mother, Sirria, his sister, Nadia, her husband, Bassem Choukair, and their three children – Mierna, Fatima and Zainab] 13 April 2022.'

The Chairman **Moore-Bick** *enters with a small crutch on his right forearm, which he places on the floor beside the right of his desk as he sits.*

Millett   Mr Chairman, can I now call, please, Mr Hisam Choucair.

Moore-Bick   Thank you. Good morning, Mr Choucair.

Choucair   Good morning sir.

Moore-Bick   You are going to take the oath, I understand.

Next to you you'll find a copy of the Koran,

And the words are on the screen, so would you read them out please?

Choucair (*sworn*)   I swear by Allah that the evidence I shall give shall be the truth, the whole truth and nothing but the truth.

Moore-Bick   Thank you very much. Do sit down and make yourself comfortable.

Yes Mr Millett.

Millett   Mr Choucair. You had a strong connection to Grenfell Tower because a number of your family members lived there?

Choucair   That's correct.

Millett   [Your sister] Nadia, and her husband, Bassem, moved into flat 193 in March 2006; is that right?

Choucair   It does sound correct.

Millett   And your sister and Bassem had three children, who were your nieces, Mierna, Fatima and Zainab.

Choucair   That's correct.

Millett   The date we have is March 2013 for when your mother, Sirria, moved into flat 191.

Choucair   That's correct.

Millett   I think it's right that you would visit your family regularly in the tower.

Choucair   That's correct.

Millett   Yes. I would like to turn to the events of [14] June 2017 after you arrived at the scene, let's have that up on the screen [your] first witness statement, paragraph 45, page 11 {IWS00001197/11} – that you heard your phone ringing at about 2.48 am?

Choucair   I think it was actually 2.45 – around that time.

Millett   Right. And you say: 'I remember thinking "Who would ring me at this time?" I am actually surprised that I woke up at all as I am quite a heavy sleeper. On answering my phone my brother, Nabil, said to me "Hisam, put on the TV. Grenfell Tower is on fire. I'm heading down there now."' So was that the first time you heard about the fire?

Choucair   That's correct.

Millett   And then you and I think your wife and your children made your way down to the tower.

Choucair   That's correct.

Millett   Yes. I think you also say in the next paragraph that from the moment that you left your flat, you tried to call your sister, Nadia, and your mother, Sirria, and Bassem a number of times.

Choucair   That's correct.

Millett   And that it rang and rang and you couldn't get a response; is that right?

Choucair   That's correct.

Millett   Then you go on to say that you arrived – this is page 12 {IWS00001197/12}, if we go to paragraph 47, about halfway down that paragraph – you arrived at the scene at 3 am. That's right, is it?

Choucair   Yes, that's correct.

Millett   How would you describe the scene when you arrived?

Choucair   I could hear a helicopter in the sky. I couldn't see it in the sky. There was hardly no one on the streets. It was a hot, humid day. I ran down Ladbroke Grove. I could hear sirens of ambulances and police cars and fire engines. As I became – as I came closer to the tower, the sound got louder and louder.

When I got to Bramley Road, it was quite chaotic. It was really loud. There were a lot of ambulances parked up, but with no one in them. The doors were all shut. There was a lot of people in the streets. People were shocked, traumatised, crying. It was chaos. There was police there and, if I'm correct, there was a cordon that they had taped off, and it was just chaos, basically.

Millett   Do you remember whether there were any officials there, other than emergency services, directing people to where they should go or how they should go about getting information?

Choucair   No, there were no officials, nobody from the TMO [Tenant Management Organisation], nobody from the government, no one from the council. There was nobody there. It was just the community residents and bereaved and survivors.

Millett   If you are shown, please, page 13
{IWS00001197/13}, in these two paragraphs, 52 and 53,
you describe how you asked for permission from two police
officers to be let through the cordon so that you could search
rescue centres but were not allowed. Is that right?

Choucair   That's correct. When I got to the cordon, the
police were really loud, telling us to get back, like as if we
were there to riot. They were shouting with an aggressive-
toned voice, and they clearly were not allowing anyone
through. I had my children with me. My children were
scared from the sounds that was going on, caused them to
cry, because obviously I have seen the Tower on fire and they
saw that as well, so they were exposed to that trauma.

Millett   Did any of the officers you spoke to provide you
with any information, to people in your position [who] were
looking for loved ones who might be in the tower, and give
you any help on that score?

Choucair   No, no police officers on the cordon, despite
myself explaining to them that we had family members on
the 22nd floor, who were obviously disabled and had
medical health issues and mobility issues, none of them
helped us to say, for example, 'I will pass this message on'
which is the reason why I demanded to speak to the person
in charge of the scene. Because I had an advance picture of
the tower by looking at the TV, so I saw the tower from all
angles, and I clearly saw that the London Fire Brigade
didn't have the tower under control – I could see they had
lost control over the tower which is why there was a – it was a
matter of urgency for me to go through that cordon.

Millett   Was there a system in place for deciding who
should be let through the cordon to get to the rescue centres
within the cordon?

Choucair   No, there was no system in place, otherwise the
officer, despite me explaining to him that our family lived in
the tower, they would have let us through otherwise, if there
was a system.

Millett   Did you have a thought about who should be running things, who should be in control, monitoring what was going on?

Choucair   Yes.

Millett   Who was that?

Choucair   I would expect someone from government or the council to have some sort of system in place, some sort of . . . order, if you know what I mean. I was expecting some sort of order in place in order to assist us, to take that burden from us, to ease the process of us looking for our loved ones.

And the reason why I'm expectant of this is because I've worked for Transport for London for many years, and we've dealt with many major incidents, fatalities, and this is something that is naturally – there's a process in place, should an event like this happen, we've liaised with emergency services, with the police, with the Home Office, with the ambulance, with the NHS. This isn't nothing new to me. So I was expectant of something like a process, a system in place to be there, but it wasn't, and I was ashamed, but I didn't have time to take that up further at that time of moment.

Millett   Now, after you had visited various rest centres, I think you then started a process of visiting a number of hospitals; is that right?

Choucair   That's correct.

Millett   Yes. I think you and [your brother] Nabil made a list of all the hospitals you could think of in the Kensington and Chelsea area and in central London, is that right?

Choucair   Yes.

Millett   Now, I think the first hospital you visited was in Paddington, the St Mary's Hospital, and you tell us in this statement, if we go, please, to paragraph 111 {IWS00001851/22}, at about 7.30 am; is that correct?

Choucair   That's correct.

Millett   Was it there that you were asked by a nurse to fill in a form with your name, address, contact number and the details of your family?

Choucair   Yes. They made me fill in a form. It asked for who I was, contact number, it asked for details about the person who we were enquiring about. I had to provide their names, the address, contact numbers, and dates of birth. Once I gave them that information, I was told to take a seat and wait. There was, again, nobody from the council, nobody from government, there were no police there, and the reception area was deserted. I was the only one there.

Moments later, a family member – other family members came through, and they were clearly traumatised and shaken, and when they were liaising with the nurse in the reception, they were struggling, and other family members had to speak on their behalf because they were quite shaken up and traumatised.

Millett   You say you were waiting; what were you waiting for?

Choucair   Further information.

Millett   From the hospital?

Choucair   That's correct. It was – I think I was – after about 40 to 45 minutes, I don't know, I became frustrated and I demanded answers. I went back to the reception area, after having comforted and liaised with other family members. I felt this wasn't acceptable. We received information that people from Grenfell Tower had been brought into the hospital, but they didn't know – the hospital were not able to identify them.

The TV was on and the police Casualty Bureau number came up, and it was on the bottom of the screen, a long number. It was clearly said on TV that this would be the number to ring if people wanted information. It was an ideal opportunity for me. I rang it and it just rang and rang and rang. I then tried again, and I got a message, an automated message, which said, 'There are no callers available to take your call'. To get that response, that there were no call handlers available to take your call, was shocking.

Millett   Mr Choucair, after St Mary's, I think you then went to the A&E department at Hammersmith Hospital; is that right?

Choucair   Yes. I asked if they had any patients who had come in from the Grenfell Tower fire. They said 'No, sorry.'

Millett   I think you then went to Charing Cross Hospital. There, as you say, you were told that they couldn't tell you whether anybody from Grenfell Tower was there due to data protection laws; is that right?

Choucair   That's correct.

Millett   What did you think about that?

Pause.

Choucair   I think silence tells you the answer. I, erm, I was very angry. I couldn't believe, despite the urgency of the situation, that I would get a response like that. I felt like as if I was being obstructed, and empathy, humanity, lack of consideration, wasn't taken into . . .

Millett   I think in the end you got an answer, and that was that your family wasn't there?

Choucair   Yes.

Millett   You say that you then visited the Chelsea and Westminster, and in your statement at paragraphs 123 to 126 {IWS00001851/24} you explain in detail what happened there. They made you wait and you were asked to fill in a form by a staff member.

Choucair   This was a frustrating experience for me. I had the same challenges with regards to data protection. It was like repeated trauma, and it was like punishment, and it was like as if your – the inside of your gut was being ripped up, and, you know, it was that sort of feeling. The lack of communication, the lack of updates, the challenges.

Millett   Was there anybody there from the Royal Borough of Kensington and Chelsea or Tenant Management Organisation in an active role, actually doing something?

Choucair   No.

Millett   Is it right that you visited some eleven hospitals and contacted the police numbers you were given, and gave your number face-to-face to the police on at least two occasions, but had received no information or updates about your family by the time you went home [at 4 pm]?

Choucair   We didn't get no update from the police. Nobody from the TMO or the council called us, despite having our numbers.

Millett   Now let's turn then to the days after the 14th June in paragraph 139 of your statement on page 27 you say there – It's difficult to be clear about the order of events in the days which followed I think that the onus was mainly on me and Nabil in terms of searching and calling the hospitals. I remember how Nabil and I would go down to the Grenfell Tower very early in the morning people of all faiths and backgrounds were there unloading food water clothes accessories into the centres and giving them out on the streets.

Choucair   It was something amazing that I had never seen before, and it put the local authority to shame, because it showed that the community were such a tight knit that they didn't rely or need the help of the council.

That feeling remained with me, and until today still remains with me, of how these crooks can – are still hiding until today and blaming each other of the events of what occurred on that day.

Millett   You tell us in your statement at [page 27] paragraph 140 {IWS00001851/27} that you chose photographs of your family and put them on sticks and appealed on live television. Did you receive any calls in response about your family, after having put up the images?

Choucair   No. And there was in the alleyway, I think it is just after the Latimer Christian Centre, there's an alleyway where people took comfort in writing on the walls, and somebody, I don't know who, put a white T-shirt of our family all on one shirt and hanged it up on the railing, and there was a Liverpool scarf on it which said, 'You'll never walk alone', and it was like 'Rest in peace', and there were messages, and people took comfort in that wall.

It was such a particular space that people were writing on the wall and showing their expressions and emotions, and took comfort in that. The adrenaline of wanting to find our loved ones was the main focus.

Millett   During that first week after 14 June, did you have any contact from the council or from the TMO at all about your loved ones?

Choucair   I didn't get no call from the council. I believe on day 4 or day 5, I'm not too sure, we did get a call from the police, and that's when we were introduced to our family liaison officers. They wanted DNA, and they introduced themselves.

Millett   When did you eventually find out that your loved ones and your family had perished in the fire?

Choucair   I don't know if it was a couple of weeks later or a couple of months later, we were – we received information. I think my mum was the first person, if I'm correct, to be identified through DNA.

Millett   Were you aware of any psychosocial or counselling support offered to you during that first week?

Choucair   No. I wasn't made aware of any counselling or social support available to me.

Slide: 'From the published Phase One Report of the Grenfell Tower Inquiry
SIR MARTIN MOORE-BICK
Chairman of the Inquiry
30 October 2019'.

Moore-Bick   The principal reason why the flames spread so rapidly up, down and around the building was the presence of the aluminium composite material (ACM) rainscreen panels with polyethylene cores, which acted as a source of fuel.

The fire is most likely to have entered the cladding as a result of hot smoke impinging on the UPVC [unplasticised polyvinyl chloride] window jamb, causing it to deform and collapse and thereby provide an opening into the cavity between the insulation and the ACM cladding panels through which flames and hot gases could pass.

The presence of polyisocyanurate (PIR) and phenolic foam insulation boards behind the ACM panels, and perhaps components of the window surrounds, contributed to the rate and extent of vertical flame spread.

It is clear that the use of combustible materials in the external wall of Grenfell Tower, principally in the form of the ACM rainscreen cladding, but also in the form of combustible insulation, was the reason why the fire spread so quickly to the whole of the building.

Slide: 'From the evidence of:
ADRIAN PARGETER
Kingspan (Insulation) Research and Development 2009–2014
Head of Marketing 2014–2015
Head of Technical and Marketing June 2015–
7–9 December 2020'.

7 December 2020.

Millett   Good Morning Mr Pargeter. Let's look at paragraph 2.7 of your first statement, please, at the bottom of page 4 {KIN00000494/4}, which I think is on the page in front of us. You say: 'In November 2014 I was promoted to Head of Marketing at Kingspan.'

At the top of page 5 [you say] that you were responsible for Kingspan's fire safety compliance campaign regarding the use of K15 in rainscreen specifications.

[At paragraph 2.8] 'In June 2015 I was appointed into the new role of Head of Technical and Marketing.'

Once you discovered in 2016 that what was being sold was not what had been tested, did you take any steps to inform the market by revising your product literature?

Pargeter   No, I didn't.

Millett   Did you realise from late 2016 that you were continuing to market K15 for compliant use above 18 metres on the basis of the 2005 test, which by then you knew had been done on a different product?

Pargeter   Yes, I was aware that was still in the literature.

Millett   And that was clearly misleading literature, wasn't it?

Pargeter   I don't think it was misleading, certainly not deliberately.

Millett   You say not deliberately, but given that you knew that the products were different and the customers did not, why not tell them candidly that, although the 2005 test was done on a different product, you do not believe that the new product would perform any differently, so that the customer would know precisely what it is they were buying?

Pargeter   That could have been a course of action, but it's not one that I did take. I believe they were getting the same performance from the 2005 product as they were getting from the 2016 product.

Millett   And that was a belief based on no science, no independent assessment and no test?

8 December 2020.

Millett   Your attitude at the time [was] that any weakness in fire safety legislation was essentially fair game to be taken advantage of in order to make sales?

Pargeter   No, not at all.

Millett   That's not how you saw it?

Pargeter   No.

Millett   Mr Pargeter, can we now please go to {KIN0007445}. I'm hoping what appears is a redacted version of this document, and I only need to look at the first part of it.

This is [9 November 2016] on an instant messenger chat between two of your technical team:

'LOL!
WHAT.
We lied?
Honest opinion now.
Yeahhhh.
Tested [Kingspan] K15 as a whole – got class 1.
Wheyy.
Shit product.
Scrap it.
But don't tell anyone that.
What like the literature?
Fire Performance.
Ha ha.
Fire Performance.
Woops.
Fire Performance.
Whey.
Look who knows their shit.

Yeah all lies mate.
Just tickling your balls mate.
BALLS!
All we do is lie in here.
Aye.'

Millett   'All we do is lie in here' – I mean, these messages were clearly never meant to see the light of day, but when he says that, it was, I have to put to you, a true, if pithy, summary of Kingspan's culture at the time.

Pargeter   I don't believe that's true at all.

Millett   That was what was happening in your technical department under your tutelage?

Pargeter   No, I disagree with that absolutely.

Millett   You had been in charge of this department for some two and a half years by this point; how do you account for this attitude to occur?

Pargeter   I can't, because that's not a culture that I endorse or foster at all.

Millett   Do you accept that a culture of lying about the fire safety of products is particularly serious, because you're taking risks with people's lives and the safety of their homes?

Pargeter   Yeah, I don't believe that we are lying. I think that they've . . . I can't explain why they're describing it as such in that way between the two of them.

9 December 2020.

Millett   The reality, Mr Pargeter, is that Kingspan's position, even in 2018 in the face of a government investigation into fire safety after Grenfell, was doing its best to ensure that the science was secretly perverted for financial gain. That is the position, isn't it?

Pargeter   That's not the position at all, no.

Millett   And that had been your own approach and Kingspan's general approach for years.

Pargeter   I disagree.

Millett   And it's still going on.

Pargeter   No, I disagree.

Slide: 'From the evidence of:
DEBORAH FRENCH
UK Sales Manager for Arconic Oct 2007–Dec 2014
9–11 February 2021
Hearing on Zoom due to Covid lockdown.'

9 February 2021.

Millett   Today we begin taking the evidence of Arconic witnesses. Arconic was the manufacturer and the seller of the rainscreen panels that were installed as the cladding on Grenfell Tower. The product was Reynobond ACM 55 PE.

Moore-Bick   Ms French, I think you're there waiting to be questioned. Can you see me and can you hear me?

French   Yes, I can, sir.

Moore-Bick   Good, thank you very much. Do you have a New Testament with you or a Bible that contains the New Testament? Now on the screen in front of you, you may find the words of the oath. (*Project text of oath on screen.*) Are they there?

French   Yes.

Moore-Bick   Would you take the bible in the right hand please and repeat the words on the screen.

French   I swear by Almighty God that the evidence I shall give shall be the truth, the whole truth and nothing but the truth.

Slide goes out.

Moore-Bick   Thank you very much. Just a couple of house-keeping matters. Can you confirm that you are alone in the room?

French   Yes I can confirm that.

Moore-Bick   Can you confirm that your mobile phone is in another room and that you don't have any other electronic device in the room which is capable of receiving messages?

French   No I have nothing in the room.

Moore-Bick   Thank you very much indeed. So Mr Millett when you're ready.

Millett   Now Miss French you made two witness statements and they will appear in the screen in front of you.

If we look at your first witness statement {MET00019063}, please, I would like to go to paragraph 2. You say: 'Between October 2007 and December 2014 my job title was UK Sales Manager for Alcoa Architectural Products SAS [which we will call Arconic] based in Merxheim, France.'

Can we start with [the managing director of Arconic] Claude Wehrle's witness statement {MET00053190/8}, page 8 please, paragraph 29. He says there in the third line: 'I was not aware before the Grenfell Tower fire that the UK remained as a predominantly PE market, up to and including 2017. I had no specific knowledge of the UK market . . .'

Is it correct that Claude Wehrle didn't know, as he maintains, as we've shown you, that the UK market was a predominantly PE market until the fire at Grenfell in 2017?

French   It's difficult for me to answer that question. I don't know what he would have known or not known. But I would say that predominantly it was PE [Polyethylene].

Millett   If we please go to the top of page 49 {MET00053173/49}, we can see:

'Debbie, Thanks for looking into this. Could you please provide me with some technical details regarding the FR [fire retardant] core particularly how it compares to the PE core. We would like to make sure that we can specify this without problems.'

Now, that's the question that you were asked [in September 2011]. Did you ever explain to your customers in terms that PE would burn?

French   I don't recall specifically explaining that to them.

Millett   Was that not something that you felt it important to explain to your customers?

French   It's not something I explained to them. If I'd been asked the question, I would have explained it, or I would have sought the right information to go and be able to explain it to them.

Millett   How much attention did you really pay to the fire safety of Reynobond 55 [PE cored ACM cladding] when you were selling it to your customers?

French   Not very much. It was not – it was very, very, very rare for a customer to raise any questions about it. It was not something that was discussed.

10 February 2021.

Millett   Let's look at the email [Richard Geater – a supplier of ACM] sends [to other fabricators] which gets passed to you and you pass on within Arconic up the chain {MET00053158_Para10/157}.

'Hi, you may or may not have seen the recent press coverage of a building fire in [November 2012] in Dubai clad in ACM?'

When you got this email and then passed it up the chain, did you read it?

French   Yes, I probably did at the time, but again, I don't recall it, it's a long time ago.

Millett   No, I understand that, but I just want to confirm that –

French   I wouldn't have not – I wouldn't have not read it, no.

Millett   Right. Okay. Can we then go to the third paragraph in the italics. It says: 'The trouble is that the cladding system here in particular but all over in general, using PE, is like a chimney which transports the fire from bottom to top or vice versa within shortest time.'

Then if you look at the fourth paragraph, 'Half of the country is full of this rubbish due to price. We have taken random samples and done a live test in Bangkok in front of architects, they almost fainted. Indeed, this panel is a whole cheat and burns fiercely.'

Did you read that message specifically?

French   I'm pretty sure I would have done, but I don't recall reading it or even recognise it now.

Millett   Would it be right to conclude from the fact that you sent it on up the chain to senior people in Arconic that you regarded it as an important message?

French   Yes.

Millett   Were you shocked?

French   I don't recall – I can't remember what my response would have been, but, as I say, having passed it on up, I was obviously concerned about it.

Millett   Did you appreciate that there was a view, at least expressed in this email, that a ventilated façade with a polyethylene-cored panel could transport fire up a building like a chimney?

French   I probably wouldn't have taken that element on board, not being a – having any knowledge of design.

Millett   Did you note his [earlier] view or observation that the recycled PE burns like paper?

French   I don't recall.

Millett   What about the observation that architects, when shown a live test, almost fainted?

French   Again, I don't recall the specifics in that.

Millett   Right. Really I'm just trying to get a feel for your reaction when you saw this email for the first time. Did it occur to you at that moment that PE-cored ACM was not fire-safe?

French   Again, I can't comment on how I would have felt. I've obviously sent it to Merxheim for a reason, and would have expected them to, you know, comment as appropriate, and if it was affecting what we were doing here, then I would have had the necessary information.

Millett   Did it occur to you, from reading this, that PE-cored ACM might be dangerous?

French   Probably not, no.

11 February 2021.

Millett   Why did Reynobond not remove PE from the market, you [said]: 'It was the cost implications.' Could you just help me, by cost implications, what did you mean?

French   The fact that we would have had to have supplied FR [fire retardant] at a more expensive rate.

Millett   Who told you that?

French   Because the cost – the difference between FR and PE were – there was a cost difference between PE and FR.

Millett   So does that mean that you would have made smaller margins if you had only been selling FR?

French   Well, I wasn't involved in the margins.

Millett   No, but clearly you had got the impression from somewhere that the reason why Reynobond was not removed from the market was cost implications.

French   Yes.

Millett   Right. So do we take it from that as a general point that, to the best of your recollection, the reason why Arconic did not withdraw its Reynobond 55 PE panel from the market was because of commercial considerations?

French   I mean, as I say, yes.

Millett   Yes. Do you recall whether, in considering those commercial considerations, any consideration was given to the fire safety consequences of continuing to sell Reynobond PE?

French   I don't recall any conversations of that nature.

Slide: 'From the published Phase One Report of the Grenfell Tower Inquiry
SIR MARTIN MOORE-BICK
Chairman of the Inquiry
30 October 2019'.

Moore-Bick   The fire on the outside of the building quickly entered many flats and smoke spread rapidly through the interior of the building. As a result, effective compartmentation was lost at an early stage. Compartmentation failed because: a. The intensity of the heat was such that the glass in the windows inevitably failed, allowing the fire to penetrate flats.

b. Extractor fan units in the kitchens had a propensity to deform and become dislodged, providing a point of entry. A number of key fire protection measures inside the tower failed. Although some fire doors held back the smoke, others did not. Some were left open and failed to close because they lacked effective self-closing devices; others were broken down by fire-fighters or wedged open with fire-fighting equipment.

Once it was clear that the fire was out of control and that compartmentation had failed, a decision should have been taken to organise the evacuation of the tower while that remained possible. The LFB continued to rely on the 'stay put' strategy in place for Grenfell Tower which was not questioned, notwithstanding all the early indications that the building had suffered a total failure of compartmentation. The 'stay put' concept had become an article of faith within the London Fire Brigade so powerful that to depart from it was . . . unthinkable.

Slide: 'From a statement by:
LESLIE THOMAS QC
on behalf of a
Bereaved Survivors Residents group
20 September 2021'.

Moore-Bick   Now, the next statement is going to be made by Professor Thomas Queen's Counsel.

Thomas   It's been said that you rise above your fears by facing them, not ignoring them. In our society, we have been brought up to respect and to be grateful for firefighters for what they do for us. They act with impressive selflessness. So our criticism of the London Fire Brigade does not detract from the individual acts of bravery of firefighters. But Grenfell is not just a story of individual heroism and bravery. It is a tragedy fraught with systemic failings, neglect and a culture of organisational obfuscation.

Fade down title slide.

Were deficiencies in the training systemic? What was the impact of austerity, cuts and deregulation on the LFB in the years preceding the Grenfell fire? How did essential communications fail at Grenfell Tower, and why was the technology so inadequate?

The LFB points the finger at the building contractors, product manufacturers, as well as the TMO [the Council's Tenant Management Organisation] and building control. Of course we do not dispute responsibility of those involved in the refurbishment and the management of Grenfell Tower.

However, the fact that others played the primary role in the causes of the fire does not absolve the LFB of its responsibilities and obligations. Can the [Bereaved, Survivors, and Residents] be confident that lessons are being learnt? Once again, the answer must be a resounding no. The link between cuts and austerity and the fire safety being compromised and eroded is real. If an organisation is understaffed and underfunded, its ability to act efficiently is likely to be compromised.

Our clients find common ground with the Fire Brigades Union on this point, whose warnings went unheard in the decades before the disaster as the London Fire Brigade experienced the worst cuts imposed on any fire service in modern history.

One of the impacts of the cuts was the reduction in staff in the control room. On the night of the fire, there were fewer control room officers on duty to handle the 999 calls and the fire survival guidance calls. There were fewer supervisors able to monitor how 999 calls were being handled and to ensure that the information was passed on the ground. In some cases, this meant that vital information about people who were trapped and could not self-evacuate was not passed on to firefighters at the tower with fatal consequences. Our clients are clear in their assertions that Prime Minister Boris Johnson, when he was the Mayor of London, had a cruel agenda of cutting the Fire Brigade's budget, firefighters' numbers and stations.

With other aspects of the LFB's inadequate response to the Grenfell Tower, the failure of communications seems to be one affected by culture that is resistant to change and innovation.

We welcome the London Fire Brigade's submissions that they have been looking into evacuation and stay put since the Grenfell Tower fire, and we too are alarmed by the continued lack of national guidance and consensus. This is a matter that is urgent and needs to be addressed at a national level. Central government must not drag its feet any longer.

Safety and lives cannot be sacrificed at the altar of austerity.

Slide: 'From the Phase 1 witness statement of:
ANDREW ROE
Assistant Commissioner, London Fire Brigade
The senior firefighter for the area at the time of the Grenfell fire
Signed statement 16/08/2017'.

Andrew Roe (*reads it standing outside the witness box*)   At about 0136, I confirmed I was mobilising to take over as the incident commander. At 0229 I arrived on scene. At 0244, I told [deputy assistant commissioner] Andy O'Loughlin that I was taking over with immediate effect. Andy confirmed that Grenfell was alight from the 3rd floor to the 24th floor with multiple people trapped inside.

At 0247 hours I asked [the Command Unit] to contact control and ask them to stop giving stay put advice if they still were. This was based on the fire spread in the building and the number of persons trapped. At the same time control asked for the same thing. I agreed and asked them to now advise people to make best efforts to escape.

Slide: 'From the evidence of:
ANDREW ROE
Commissioner of the London Fire Brigade'.

30 November 2021.

Millett   Commissioner Andrew Roe. It was as assistant commissioner [of London Fire Brigade] that you attended and indeed acted as incident commander at the Grenfell Tower fire on 14 June 2017.

Roe   That's correct.

Millett   After that fire, you were made deputy commissioner and director of operations from November 2019 then appointed commissioner in January 2020.

Roe   That is correct.

Millett   How did the LFB come to be in denial about systemic issues?

Roe   If we think of Grenfell specifically we knew that there was a potential risk of wholesale failure of compartmentation. We knew, for example, the dangers of poor maintenance and management of buildings, the very real possibility of a very large fire in London involving loss of life.

I think one of the most serious issues, not just for the London Fire Brigade but again for the service nationally, was that we were simply not scrutinised effectively over a period of decades. I think every single major institution that should have kept those, you know, survivors, the bereaved, the people who lived in the tower, safe, let the families down. It was the most appalling example of institutional failure I think in recent British history, and we were part of that as well.

Millett   Focusing in on perhaps some of the key elements, do you accept, Commissioner, that the LFB had what I might call corporate knowledge as at June 2017 of the risks posed by non-compliant façade panels in use on high-rise buildings across London?

Roe   Yes, because I think it's clear from the evidence given to this Inquiry that that was the case.

Millett   Does it follow from that that you also accept that the possibility of widespread compartmentation failure within a high-rise building was a risk that was real and known to the Brigade as at June 2017?

Roe   Yes. I think what caught people by utter surprise, and I would include myself, in the first few moments of the

Grenfell Tower fire, was just the totality of it. It seemed almost unbelievable to me that we would lose an entire residential block in modern Britain. You know, it still shocks me to this day, because I think it says something about all the systems and institutions that should have kept those people safe.

Millett   Does it follow from that answer that the risk of such widespread compartmentation failure leading to the untenability of the stayput policy in such a building is a scenario – in fact, would have been a scenario at the time – that you consider that LFB's officers should have been prepared to respond to at an incident?

Roe   I think it's of note that, you know, I think where we didn't do enough for our officers and crews was to prepare them for how they might deal with that situation, should it confront them.

Moore-Bick   Can I just ask this: I suppose the really important thing is to recognise what's happening in front of you, one of the things that was required – and maybe this is something you're now doing – is to put your immediate responders, the watch manager level, in a position to recognise a serious breach of compartmentation if it's facing them.

Roe   Yeah, I mean, we've done that now.

1 December 2021.

Millett   Your understanding at the time of the Grenfell Tower fire was that the risk of fire spread via an external façade system applied to certain buildings overseas but not in England?

Roe   I was absolutely alive to the possibility of some form of external fire spread in the UK. It wasn't a complete, you know, blind-sightedness on the possibility of some form of external fire spread. I'm talking about the total failure of a modern method of construction in the context of façades.

Millett   You looked at overseas fires, particularly in the Middle East and Europe, and said '[that] the extent of that façade fire couldn't happen here because of our regulatory regime'?

Roe   I don't think it was even as concrete as that, I just don't think I . . . well, I mean, I suppose the way I would have put that in my own head is: 'I'm not sure that could happen here', because I had enough faith in the building regulatory system that I thought it wouldn't.

Up to the point of Grenfell, I would have anticipated partial failure of that regulatory system, absolutely, because that's the nature of emergency services; you invariably pick up the pieces after some failure of a regulatory system.

I think Grenfell, you know, continues to me to be an article of public shame, really, for the United Kingdom, that our regulatory system failed so completely.

Millett   Can we go to your first Phase 2 witness statement, please {LFB00060655/9}, and let's look together, commissioner, at paragraph 20. You say that at the very end of the paragraph:

'I note that, to the best of LFB knowledge, the Grenfell Tower fire represented the first departure from the standard stay put strategy in England and Wales.'

Roe   [It] is the first known recorded time of an officer, which in this case was me, taking a recorded decision to say: the stay put strategy is no longer applicable in this residential building and therefore we must carry out a total evacuation and rescue of the block.

I'm certainly not aware of where previously, certainly in the London Fire Brigade, an incident commander had taken the recorded decision that a stay put strategy was no longer applicable to that building in its total sense.

Millett   You revoked stay put at Grenfell at 2.47, it was rescue.

Roe   Yes.

Slide: 'From a statement by:
IMRAN KHAN QC
on behalf of a Bereaved Survivors Residents group
5 July 2022'.

Photograph of Mohamed Amied 'Saber' Neda comes up on the screen.

Millett   I would now invite Mr Imran Khan QC to come to the podium, please, to make the presentation on behalf of Mohamed Saber Neda from flat 205 on floor 23.

I should just say that the statements and the materials that will be discussed or displayed during this presentation may be distressing to some, and they may wish to absent themselves from the room.

Moore-Bick   Thank you very much. Mr Khan, yes, please.

Slide fades down.

Khan   Good morning, sir. This is an incredibly difficult and distressing time, and the image that was just displayed was of Mohamed Amied Neda.

I hope that what I say today does justice to the memory of Mr Neda, and gives some comfort to his family, who are here today, Farhad and Shakila.

Mohamed Amied Neda was affectionately known as Saber. Saber in Persian means patience. And it described Mr Neda to a tee; he was the epitome of patience.

He was born in Afghanistan. He was a loving husband to Shakila, a father to his son, Farhad. He died aged 57 on 14 June 2017. He lived with his wife and his son in flat 205 on the 23rd floor, their tenancy of the flat commencing [in] 1999.

Saber met his wife, Shakila, in 1989, when they were 28 and 26 respectively. At the time, he was a high-ranking officer in the Afghan army. They married in the wonderful city of

Kabul in 1991, and were husband and wife for over 27 years. Shakila says it was 'a marriage full of love'.

Unfortunately, Saber and his family had to flee Afghanistan in 1998 because of the risk they faced from the Taliban. He, Saber, was targeted as an army officer, and Shakila, who was a primary school teacher, was no longer able to work as the Taliban had closed the school where she was employed. The family, like many, sought refuge in the UK, and came to London in March 1998, where they were able to claim asylum.

Saber was a hardworking individual, and took whatever work he could find to support his family, including as a minicab driver.

Saber and his [wife Shakila and son Farhad] had arrived home at 00.52, just moments before the outbreak of the fire. They had spent a wonderful evening with Shakila's sister and family in Heston, having gone there to break their fast, as, sir, you will recall that it was Ramadan at the time. When they arrived home, the lifts were working. All three went up to their flat in the lift. Both Farhad and Shakila recalled hearing loud noises from the extractor/ventilator fan immediately upon exiting the lift on the floor. Shakila recalls telling her husband that they should report the noise to the TMO as it was so loud and they would not be able to sleep.

Farhad in fact telephoned the TMO and was told that an engineer was on his way to fix it. He also recalls being told that the Fire Brigade were also coming.

Upon realising that there was a fire, they went onto their landing to investigate, and saw their neighbours from flat 206.

They also saw a lot of people from the lower floors coming up the stairs in a state of panic, and telling them that there was a fire and they had been told to go up to the top floor.

Four people came into the Nedas' flat seeking refuge from the fire. The others went into the adjoining flats on the 23rd floor.

Farhad said that the presence of people coming up and those who said there was a fire further below, together with the fact they had been told by the LFB to go up, influenced his family's decision to go back into their flat.

On one occasion, Farhad is very clear that he spoke to a firefighter, as one of his friends outside the tower passed their phone so he could speak to one of them directly. Farhad says the firefighter's response was – and I now quote from what he says – that they were making their way up – that is firefighters – and had reached a certain level, but he did not know which, and they were on their way up. The firefighter told Farhad: 'He told me we should stay in the flat, he told me to stay put.'

Meanwhile, [they all] looked out of the kitchen window and, in desperation, signalled with the lights and screens on their phones to attract the attention of emergency services on the ground.

But by 02.00 hours the fire had entered the front bedroom, situated at the front door. Saber instructed everyone to stay away from the bedroom and for all of them to gather in the kitchen.

Thick smoke filled the flat. They soaked towels and filled water bottles. Quite horrifically, Shakila felt that she had no option but to throw herself out of the window, saying that she did not want to be burnt alive.

She believes this to be around 2.00 am. She says she was pulled back by Saber and Farhad, and it was at this point they agreed they had no option but to try and leave and make their way down.

Farhad took his mother and left the flat after placing wet towels over their faces. Saber told his wife and son that he would be right behind them as they left. Saber stayed behind to offer assistance to the Elgwahry and Afrasiabi families. This was, Chair, members of the panel, the last time that Shakila and Farhad saw their husband and father. They believed Saber was behind them with the four women, and their last sight of him alive was seeing him helping the women with the wet towels.

Farhad and Shakila made their way out down the stairs through thick, black, choking smoke, Farhad carrying and dragging his mother out, believing Saber was somewhere behind them. Shakila called out to Saber when they reached the stairwell door, but he didn't answer. She attempted to go back to him, but Farhad told her they would not make it out of the tower if they turned back.

We also know that upon returning home, Saber's brother-in-law, Habibrahman Abdulrahman, found a voice message on his phone from Saber, in which he said this:

'Goodbye, I am leaving this world, goodbye. I hope you won't be in pain. Goodbye, everyone.'

This was the last message he left before he died. We're told that his voice was calm and he didn't show any fear.

Because of her mobility issues, Farhad had to carry his mother by clasping her around the waist with one arm and around his shoulders.

Farhad had told his mother that there were twelve steps on each staircase and twenty-four steps for each floor. She has said that she could feel something beneath her feet as they were going down the stairs. When she asked Farhad what it was, he told her not to worry, it's just the fire hoses. The firefighters were still coming, coming up. He told his mother to be careful and he hugged her close to him. He put his hand on her shoulder and told her that he was with her. Farhad said to his mother, 'Just stay with me'.

Shakila recalls that around the 18th floor she stumbled and Farhad turned on the light of his mobile telephone. He only kept it on for a few minutes because he didn't want to drain the battery. The light wasn't particularly helpful because it was pitch black smoke, but what it did show, in shocking, graphic detail, was the sight of people lying motionless on the stairs. Farhad kept the light on for a few minutes so they could see where they were placing their feet to avoid stepping on people. Shakila says, perhaps thankfully, they didn't see the faces or any identifying features of those who were on the stairs. It was very difficult to see through the thick black smoke. She did however say this to her son, as it dawned on her that they were not walking over hose pipes, they were walking over dead and dying people.

At that point, Farhad had no choice now but to carry his severely disabled mother down the stairs on his back. She could no longer walk. Shakila says this of their walk down night: 'I would never have had any chance at all of getting out of the tower if it were not for the incredible strength and love of my son.'

We know that no firefighter managed to reach the 23rd floor, and despite the repeated advice of the emergency services to multiple occupants on this floor that firefighters were making their way to them, no dedicated BA [breathing apparatus] crew was deployed to the 23rd floor until after 02.08, and none reached the floor.

At 02.40 hours approximately a male had been seen to fall from the mid to upper floors, landing within the children's play area to the west of the tower. With the assistance of a colleague and firefighters, this individual was moved to a place of safety, where paramedics could attend to him.

A paramedic quickly confirmed there were no signs of life. We now know, sir, that this was Saber.

The post-mortem report concludes that Saber died from 'multiple injuries consistent with fall from height'.

Professor Purser, in his evidence to the Inquiry, said
this: 'Mr Neda fell from the tower with 20 per cent [carboxy-
haemoglobin] in his blood at the time he fell. If [Mr Neda]
waited and then decided to walk down, following his son and
his wife, there was a good chance he would have not been
able to walk all the way down, he would have collapsed on
the way down'.

Farhad has said this about the last time he saw his father as
he escaped with his mother: 'It is the last time my eyes set
eyes on my best friend in the world. Dad was a hero . . . He
could have come with us, at that moment. However, he did
not leave those women who were distressed and needed
help in our flat.

He died trying to save their lives, he gave them hope and
encouragement. He was calm and he did not panic.

He certainly did not put himself first and just rush out with
us. He was being composed and caring towards the four
women who had looked to him for help. He knew full well,
as did Mum and I, and those ladies, that we were all in
mortal danger.'

Interval.

Slide: 'From the evidence of:
Dr SARAH COLWELL
Employed by the Building Research Establishment since leaving
school in 1985
– Senior Scientific Officer 1995
– Business Group Manager for the Reaction to Fire Team (providing
commercial testing services in relation to fire performance) 2002
– Business Group Manager Fire Suppression Team 2009
Director: Fire Suppression Team 2016–'.

14 February 2022.

Moore-Bick   Today we're going to start hearing evidence
from Dr Sarah Colwell of the Building Research
Establishment. Yes, Ms Grange.

Grange   Yes, thank you. Dr Colwell, [full scale tests] were carried out at various times between 31 May 2001 and 14 November 2001. Why did you choose ACM PE [aluminium composite material with polyethylene core] as one of the products to be tested?

Colwell   It would have been offered to us as part of the industry interest.

Grange   What do you remember now about that test on the system incorporating ACM PE panels?

Colwell   It was a test that failed in the very early stages.

Grange   What was your reaction at the time to it doing so?

Colwell   Shocked. I was shocked at the speed it took off.

Grange   Can you remember the reaction of any others who were present at the test?

Colwell   We were all surprised.

Grange   Can we agree that, in very simple terms, this was an inferno, wasn't it?

Colwell   It was a very rapid, very large fire growth, yes.

Grange   This was a catastrophic escalation, wasn't it?

Colwell   It was a very rapid fire growth, yes.

Grange   Was there a sense of alarm at the BRE [Building Research Establishment] in the wake of this test?

Colwell   We were very surprised by that performance, yes.

Grange   What about the Department [for Communities and Local Government]. Do you remember them expressing alarm at the catastrophic escalation of this test?

Colwell   Yes, they – we were all concerned at the performance.

Grange   Were there any discussions with the Department about whether this was a suitable product that could be used to clad high-rise buildings?

Colwell   I don't believe anyone felt that it was appropriate.

Grange   Did you consider after this test [in 2001] that the use of ACM panels on a high-rise building would present nothing other than a grave risk to occupants in the event of fire?

Colwell   I genuinely – yes, I couldn't see that ACM would be an appropriate product.

Grange   So is it fair to say that you didn't consider PE-cored ACM to be suitable for external cladding applications in high-rise buildings?

Colwell   Correct.

Grange   Did anyone consider alerting industry or local authorities or building control or other building owners to this result and to the obvious dangers posed by these panels?

Colwell   How the Department chose to transmit that, I don't know.

Grange   Is the answer that – no one within the BRE thought about doing that in the light of this test?

Colwell   We would not go out and make comment around that, no.

Grange   Why not?

Colwell   We were delivering this to them to make the necessary statements and changes arising from that.

16 February 2022.

Grange   Were you aware at this point of any international cladding fires that had used ACM PE?

Colwell   There were fires around that time [the late 1990s, early 2000s], yes.

Grange   Yes. Wasn't that another reason why it would have been good to warn about such panels?

Colwell   With hindsight, it would have been appropriate.

Grange   Did Mr [Brian] Martin [of the Department for Communities and Local Government] appear to be taking your concerns seriously at [a] meeting [early in 2014]?

Colwell   Yes.

Grange   Right. Did he give you any idea about when any review of Approved Document B [on fire safety] might be, in which he would pick this up?

Colwell   Unfortunately not, and with hindsight, that's probably one of the biggest areas of concern, that we never really pushed for that clarity. Meetings of that type with Brian tended to be of a fairly informal nature.

Grange   Wasn't it quite an important meeting that the BRE ought to have been taking notes from it?

Colwell   With hindsight, yes.

Grange   Yes. Can you explain why the BRE itself didn't do something to warn industry about the dangers?

Colwell   Those would have been referred back to the Department to address. We wouldn't have stepped into that space. That wasn't something we did.

Grange   What, even if there was a real-life safety issue?

Colwell   The vehicle for dissemination and the authority of those types of statements were expected to come from the [Department].

17 February 2022.

Grange   There is an email chain between you and David Metcalfe [the director of the Centre for Window and Cladding Technology, the CWCT]. It's dated 13 March 2015. Page 2 {CWCT0000040/2} he says: 'Dear Sarah.

Around the use of combustible materials and the wording of Clause 12.7 of ADB. It was my understanding that you agreed to draft a note clarifying the intent of the clause. Has any progress been made on this? I would be grateful for a quick response.' Do you see that?

Colwell   Yes, I do.

Grange   If we go up to the next email in the chain on page 1 {CWCT0000040/1}, we can see a brief response from you on the same day, on 13 March [2015] and you say 'Hi David. Yes, a note has been drafted and revisited – it is still draft hopefully it will be closed out soon. Kind Regards, Sarah.'

Colwell   Yes.

Grange   Now, was that true? Was there a draft in existence that you thought would be closed out soon?

Colwell   The drafts that I'd discussed existed as headline notes.

Grange   Right. Why not tell Mr Metcalfe that?

Colwell   That email and the following correspondence is not as clear as it could have been or should have been.

Grange   Well, it's wholly misleading, isn't it?

Colwell   With hindsight, yes, it is.

Grange   You've actually drafted an email that suggests that positive steps are happening.

Colwell   Yes.

Grange   David Metcalfe chased for a response in writing from you on numerous dates. he chased on 18 August 2015, on 14 October, on 2 November, on 10 November. Do you remember receiving these chasing emails from Mr Metcalfe?

Colwell   Yes I'm aware that there were chasers followed. I should have contacted him directly and explained to him what was going on and I didn't.

Grange   It was you that was tasked with speaking to Brian Martin, yes?

Colwell   Yes.

Moore-Bick   Dr Colwell, one possible view is that you were deliberately stringing Mr Metcalfe along –

Colwell   I appreciate that.

Moore-Bick   And then you got to the point when you simply ignored him. What would you say about that?

Colwell   I fully accept that, on reflection, I should have closed this down much earlier and much more effectively.

Moore-Bick   Yes. All right.

Grange   There was a [Centre for Window and Cladding Technology] fire group meeting held on 17 March 2016. Let's turn up the minutes of that meeting. They're at {CLG00019440}. We can see on page 1 that you attended, as did Brian Martin.

If we go to page 2 {CLG00019440/2}, towards the bottom of the page, there is a section headed 'Combustibility of material', and we can see that reads: 'Approved Document B (Clause 12.7) requires insulation and filler material in the external walls of tall buildings to be of limited combustibility.' Do you see that?

Colwell   Yes.

Grange   Right. In your witness statement, you tell us that you can't recall whether or not Brian Martin accepted those matters. Is that still the case?

Colwell   I don't have direct recollection of who made those particular statements, no.

Grange   You'd met with Brian Martin, we know, in January 2014, when he said he was going to take it further. We're now two years on from that, over two years on.

Was there anything Brian Martin did or said at this time which led you to believe that he did consider the matter to be urgent?

Colwell   I think his acceptance that there was this need for change, for making that change happen.

Grange   Right, and did you consider it to be urgent?

Colwell   I believe by that point that it was one of the key things that needed to be changed in the revision, yes.

Grange   But did you consider it to be urgent? Not just a key change that needed to happen in the future?

Colwell   Yes, it needed to be changed.

Grange   And changed quickly; yes?

Colwell   Yeah, and – yeah, it needed to happen, yes.

Grange   Right. Now, by this time, so March 2016, were you aware of the fires at The Torch residential building in Dubai in February 2015 and at The Address Downtown Hotel in December 2015?

Colwell   Yes.

Grange   So two really significant fires had occurred in the UAE in this period; yes?

Colwell   Yes.

Grange   Did you know that those involved ACM PE?

Colwell   Yes.

Grange   In March 2016, were you still engaged in any work in the UAE in relation to their regulatory codes or anything to do with external fire spread?

Colwell   Yes, I would have been aware of that.

Grange   And you were aware, weren't you, of the fire at the Ajman Towers in Dubai on 28 March 2016?

Colwell   Yeah.

Grange   Let's look at an email to help you
{CLG10008111}. Here is a discussion about that fire
between Brian Martin [and others]. Now, you're not copied
into these emails, but if we look at the top email in the chain,
29 March 2016: 'I know [smiley face].' We can see it's about
the Ajman fire: 'Huge blaze hits UAE residential towers.'

Then in the second line: 'Sarah thinks it's burning debris
landing on balconies.' Do you see that?

Colwell   Yes.

Grange   So it would appear that you were aware of that fire
at the time. Did you know that that involved ACM PE?

Colwell   Yes.

Grange   Did any of these cladding fires alert you to the
need to provide clearer guidance to industry as a matter of
some urgency?

Colwell   As I say, I hadn't made the connection at that time
of the extent to which ACM was being used in the UK
market.

Grange   {BLM00000153/3}. It's an email sent to you by
Nick Jenkins [of Euroclad Limited] on 20 January 2016.
'Use of ACM Cladding Panels on Buildings Exceeding 18m
in Height.'

He says: 'I understand that you might be the best person to
help me with some clarification I'm seeking in relation to the
current UK regulations as they apply to wall constructions
for buildings over 18m[etres] featuring rainscreen panels
formed from ACMs?'

What was your reaction to the news that standard ACM
panels with a polyethylene core had been used and were
being supplied for use on many tall residential buildings
recently?

Colwell   Surprised.

Grange   Now, given your knowledge about the dangers of this product dating all the way back to 2001, and your more recent work in the Middle East, surely your reaction was one of horror at this point; yes?

Colwell   As I say, I was surprised, yes.

Grange   Wasn't this a red alert situation that required urgent action on your part, on the BRE's part?

Colwell   As a result of it, I referred it to the [Department], yes.

Grange   What do you mean by that?

Colwell   That email was referred on to [the Department] to follow up.

Grange   Didn't you and the BRE think at this point, 'Wow, we need to do something urgently, this is a very serious situation'? Did you speak to Brian Martin, did you pick up the phone to Brian Martin, who you knew well, and press him to do something?

Colwell   At that point, no – I forwarded Nick [Jenkin's email] to Brian. It was my understanding that the Department would take that message forward and [take] action if and as required.

Grange   Did you consider whether the BRE itself ought to put out a statement to industry alerting industry to the dangers associated with this product and the concerns that the BRE had about using it on tall residential buildings?

Colwell   No, I didn't.

Grange   Why not?

Colwell   It was not a route that BRE had taken in those circumstances. We referred it to the Department.

Grange   Why don't we see anything from the BRE about the dangers associated with ACM PE, once you know for sure at this point that it is being used on tall buildings. Why don't we see that?

Colwell   We spoke where we were invited to speak.

Grange   If we go up to the next email in the chain, we can see that you write on 12 February 2016:

'Dear Nick, I would suggest that you contact Brian Martin at the DCLG, [the Department of Communities and Local Government] (you give his email address) . . . as they are the body with responsibility for this document.'

Do you see that?

Colwell   Yes.

Grange   Then if we look at the email at the very top of page 1, we can see an internal email in which Phil Cook [of Euroclad Limited], having been informed by Nick Jenkins that you have referred to the matter, writes this: 'Nick, What a buck passing load of incompetents.'

Do you see that?

Colwell   Yes.

Grange   Do you disagree with that description, given what we've just seen?

Colwell   Given that [the Department] needed to be made aware of it and were the people able to provide the definitive guidance he was seeking I'm not quite sure why he felt that we would speak on [their] behalf.

Grange   Can you explain why we see no correspondence whatsoever before the Grenfell Tower fire in which the BRE warns the Department about the grave risk to life safety if action is not taken urgently to address the use of ACM PE in the UK market?

Colwell   Statements of that nature were not publicly made by BRE. They were referred to the Department for them to take action on.

Grange   Can you explain how that was professionally or ethically acceptable on your or the BRE's part?

Colwell   We believed that the Department were best placed to make those statements to the widest market.

Slide: 'From the evidence of:
BRIAN MARTIN
Seconded 50% of the time to the Department of Communities and Local Government (DCLG).
Then left BRE and became Principal Construction Professional at DCLG 2008–2017
Then Head of Technical Policy 2017–
17, 21, 22, 28, 30 March 2022'.

17 March 2022.

Sir Martin Moore-Bick   Today we're going to begin hearing evidence from Mr Brian Martin, the official at the former DCLG [Department for Communities and Local Government] who was responsible for the Building Regulations. Yes, Mr Millett.

Millett   You joined the BRE – Building Research Establishment in 1999. When you arrived did you get any training on fire science, fire spread, the tests?

Martin   Not any specific extra training.

Millett   Right.

Martin   I would go to the laboratories, get to know the lab technicians and the scientists, so I developed a better understanding than most building control officers would have.

Millett   Now in your witness statement you say: 'Shortly after joining BRE I was seconded to the Department as the

lead consultant on a contract to provide technical support
. . . on matters relating to fire safety.' Yes?

Martin   Yes.

Millett   So it was two to three days a week at the
Department and two to three days a week at the BRE.

Martin   Yes.

Millett   Now in September 2008 you left the BRE and you
became employed full-time by the Department and your job
title was Principal Construction Professional, yes?

Martin   Correct.

Millett   You were responsible for providing policy advice to
Ministers in relation to technical aspects of the Building
Regulations.

Martin   Yes.

Millett   Did you get any training on the Building
Regulations and the approved documents?

Martin   Not – no.

Millett   Let's move to the Garnock Court fire [in Irvine,
Scotland] in June 1999. What did you consider to be the
important aspects of the fire that you took away?

Martin   Don't use combustible cladding, I suppose, in very
simple terms, and that multiple fires in a block of flats
creates major problems for firefighters.

Millett   And presumably – did this occur to you –
challenged the very fundamental underpinning of the
stay-put policy?

Martin   Absolutely, yes.

Millett   [And] ADB [Approved Document B] did not
require non-combustible materials to be chosen for the
external wall. It would need amending? Wouldn't it?

Martin   Yeah.

Millett   Now, let's look at the report of the [House of Commons] Environment, Transport and Regional Affairs Committee. It's {CLG00019478} published [in] December 1999 [paragraph 20] – 'We believe that all external cladding systems should be required either to be entirely non-combustible, or to be proven through full-scale testing not to pose an unacceptable level of risk in terms of fire spread.'

Why did it take the Grenfell Tower fire to provoke a change which had been flagged clearly by the select committee in 1999?

Martin   I think in general if you adopted a near enough absolute requirement for non-combustibility, it's probably impracticable and unduly – unreasonably onerous.

21 March 2022.

Martin   Did it occur to you before any experimental testing [in 2001] that the use of polyethylene at height above 18 metres even at this time, might present a serious danger in the event of a fire?

Martin   No.

Millett   Was there any discussion within the BRE or within the Department on that topic at about this time?

Martin   Not that I recall, no.

Millett   Now, [in September 2002 while you were still working at the Building Research Establishment] Dr Sarah Colwell came into your office and showed you – what did she show you?

Martin   Sarah walked into the office and showed me a small piece of material which I now know to be ACM –

Millett   Right.

Martin   – and said, 'Look at this stuff, we just did a fire test on it', and she described [how] the aluminium melted away, exposed the polyethylene, and then the polyethylene began to burn.

Millett   Did she tell you she was shocked by what she saw?

Martin   My recollection is that the conversation was – it was an interesting outcome.

Millett   An interesting outcome, all right. So, if not shocking, then it stood out; can we put it that way?

Martin   Obviously in the context of this Inquiry, this sounds awful, but I think I should try and be as honest as possible: it was an interesting conversation that was – that's what I recall.

Millett   Did Sarah Colwell tell you what had happened during the test?

Martin   I don't remember.

Millett   Would you agree that the full-scale test identified aluminium with a polyethylene core [was] a catastrophic and very rapid failure?

Pause.

Martin   It's clearly very rapid. I'm not sure how you'd define catastrophic.

Millett   Did you get the feeling at the time that here was a test observed by your colleagues which shocked them or, at lowest, surprised them, and would have demonstrated that the use of ACM with a polyethylene core with [cavity wall] insulation caused an inferno?

Martin   At the time, I don't remember anyone discussing this as being a particularly unusual outcome.

Millett   When she [Sarah Colwell] brought you the piece of ACM and told you about the test, what did you think her purpose was in doing so?

Pause.

Did you have any thoughts at the time along the lines of: 'Well, we can't be having any of that above 18 metres in this country'?

Pause.

Martin I honestly don't remember thinking much more about it.

Millett But she'd brought this to you, because you were the ADB [Approved Document B] man [at the BRE in September 2002] so to speak; what did you think her purpose of bringing this to you was, other than to alert the ADM man to the result?

Martin At the time, it felt like a conversation amongst colleagues about an interesting result.

Millett Well, it's more than interesting, isn't it? This was a conflagration, a 20-metre fire. Given her reaction, as she has told us, and given the fact that she chose to discuss it with you, can you really not tell us any more than it was an interesting conversation?

Martin No. As I say, it sounds awful now, and . . .

Millett All right.

Martin That's honestly the only recollection I have of that test, that short conversation.

Millett Sarah Colwell told us – {Day232/100:16–21} – that she couldn't see that ACM would be an appropriate product for use on high-rise buildings. Now, did you discuss that topic with her at the time at any time between May 2001 and mid-September 2002?

Martin No.

Millett Did you consider yourself by September 2002 that the use of aluminium composite material panels with a polyethylene core on a high-rise building would present anything other than a grave risk to occupants in the event of a fire?

Martin   It was not something that I gave any consideration to at the time.

Millett   Can you just explain why that is so?

Martin   The opportunity never arose to have that consideration.

Millett   The Government now knew [by September 2002], if it didn't know it before, that fire safety compliance testing was either flawed or technical loopholes were being exploited by manufacturers to make false claims about fire safety?

Martin   I think that last conclusion may be going too far.

Millett   Now, it's right, I think, isn't it, that the reports and data from [these tests] have never, before this Inquiry, been released into the public domain?

Do you know who decided that these reports and the data from this work should not be disseminated outside government and the Building Research Establishment?

Martin   I'm not aware of anyone making that decision.

Millett   What about after Grenfell? I mean, when Grenfell happened, had you forgotten about these tests?

Martin   I hadn't forgotten about them. I think at some point after Grenfell I tried to track down the reports and couldn't find them.

Millett   Mr Martin, are you able to give us an assurance that you did not sit on this data or your knowledge of it for the full nine years that you were a full-time civil servant, hoping and praying fervently that it would never see the light of day?

Martin   I can assure you that [I] would [not] have done that.

Millett   Is there any innocent explanation for why this data was sat on between September 2002 and disclosure to the Inquiry?

Martin   Tragically, I think it just got forgotten and fell between the gaps.

Millett   How could it possibly have been forgotten, given what it showed?

Martin   I've been asking myself that question for quite some time.

Millett   The guidance in ADB was supposed to state the Secretary of State's intention in clear terms which everybody can understand; yes?

Martin   Yes.

Millett   If ADB [Approved Document B] remained misleading or open to interpretation, then the Secretary of State's intention here would be confounded?

Martin   Yes.

Millett   Yes. And that risk was a potentially lethal risk?

Martin   Yes.

Millett   Was there any reason at this stage, March 2004, for you to think that any part of ADB [Approved Document B] was at that time misleading or open to interpretation?

Martin   Fire safety is a very subjective subject. It's very difficult to be categorical about everything.

22 March 2022.

Millett   Now, the Red Tape Challenge was a cross-government policy [of the Coalition Government] about which existing regulations should be improved, kept or scrapped. Did you consider applying for an exemption for the Building Regulations from the Red Tape Challenge process?

Martin   No –

Millett   And why not?

Martin   We didn't really have a strong argument for doing so.

Millett   Well, how about life safety being a strong argument for doing so?

Martin   Well, Building Regulations covers a wide range of different things. In terms of the Red Tape Challenge, it was looking to reduce unnecessary – what I think the government would have considered unnecessary – burden. So, arguably, if there was a provision which would have a negative impact on safety, then I think the Government wouldn't have supported that.

Millett   [Going back to Approved Document B] why not at this stage [February 2016] go out with [an] interim measure, such as an FAQ [Frequently Asked Questions guidance], and clarify, in unambiguous terms, paragraph 12.7 [of Approved Document B dealing with fire safety]?

Martin   Yeah, I think at this time we'd really struggled to get anything done within the Department following the coalition government taking over after the financial crisis, there was a lot of pressure on the team in relation to deregulation. 'Regulation' was a dirty word and any document that would have gone out from the Department would have needed to have had political approval.

Millett   Are you saying that even posting an FAQ on the Department's website would have needed ministerial approval?

Martin   Oh yes.

Millett   Really?

Martin   Absolutely, yeah. Yeah, it's a document published by the Department – anything like that is politically cleared.

Millett   So I think we can take it that you didn't, after March 2016, make any senior official or minister aware that you had accepted that an important section of the statutory guidance, in place for almost a decade, was misleading?

Martin   Not specifically.

Millett   Did you give any consideration to investigating the potential impact of having left in place for almost a decade guidance on external fire spread within Approved Document B which, by 2016, you had come to accept was misleading, unclear, and open to interpretation?

Martin   No, I don't think I did consider that.

28 March 2022.

Millett   Can we look at {SWE00000001}, please, a witness statement from Sam Webb, who has provided this statement to the Inquiry this year, 2022. Sam Webb is an architect and a longstanding member of the RIBA [Royal Institute of British Architects] Council from 1973 to 2012. He has had a long career in the health and safety field and produced a report following the Lakanal [fire in Camberwell, South London in 2009 in which six people died].

Page 90 of this statement {SWE00000001/90}, please. Here in page 90 he's covering various individuals that he came across in the context of Lakanal he says this at 23.10: 'Brian Martin: I sat next to Brian Martin at lunch in the Cholmondeley Room in the Palace of Westminster at an APPG [All-Party Parliamentary Group] Event on 9 February 2016.'

He goes on: 'I put the following to him. If ADB wasn't rewritten in clear language as the Lakanal Coroner had recommended to the Minister in her Rule 43 letter, then another fire like Lakanal was inevitable. If it happened in the middle of the night when people were asleep then the death toll was likely to be ten-to-twelve times the six people who died in the Lakanal fire.'

'Brian Martin's reply to me was, "Where's the evidence?
Show me the bodies".'

'This was over a year before the Grenfell Tower fire. The
impression I gained from Brian Martin was if it hasn't
happened then it wouldn't happen. It was as if he needed a
disaster before he or the Government would act.'

Do you remember discussing with [Mr Webb] the coroner's
recommendations from the Lakanal inquest?

Martin   I do have some recollection of that conversation,
yes.

Millett   Do you remember him saying to you that if ADB
wasn't rewritten in clear language, as the coroner had
recommended, then another fire like Lakanal was inevitable
and many more might die if the fire occurred at night?

Martin   He probably said something along those lines. He
seems to have a very accurate memory of exactly what words
he used.

Millett   Well, that's a comment on his statement, but I'm
just asking you for your recollection.

Martin   I think I was explaining to him that I was working
in a situation where, in order to justify imposing higher
standards, then there was a very high bar to address. We
would need to demonstrate that any changes were not only
cost – as a minimum cost-effective, but also meet the one in
– I think it was one in, three out by then rules.

So what I was trying to explain to him is: it would be difficult
to justify raising standards, given that what we were actually
experiencing was, you know, a regular reduction in the
number of fire deaths.

Millett   Did you say to him, 'Where's the evidence? Show
me the bodies'?

Martin   I wouldn't have said that.

Millett   Did you use words to that effect?

Martin   No, I think I'd have used words to the effect I've just given you. I mean, government policy was – had progressively hardened over quite an extensive period, the one in, one out thing. I think the Prime Minister described people like me as an enemy of enterprise.

30 March 2022.

Millett   Looking back on your time, going back to 1999, is there anything that you would have done differently?

Martin   Yes, sir. I find it difficult to express how sorry I am for what's happened to the people of Grenfell Tower. Over the last few months, I've been looking through the evidence and the documents, and it became clear to me that I could have potentially prevented this happening.

I think I'd become entrenched in a position where I was focused on what I could do to improve the approved document [B, on fire safety], and didn't realise just how big the problem was. I think at the meeting in 2014 with the CWCT [Centre for Window and Cladding Technology]. If I'd been there in the second part of the meeting, with Dr Colwell there, I think between the two of us perhaps we would have realised how severe the risk really was and I would have escalated the issue.

What I will say is that the approach the government – the successive governments – had to regulation had had an impact on the way we worked, the resources that we had available, and perhaps the mindset that we'd adopted as a team, and I think, as a result of that, I ended up being the single point of failure in the Department, and I think that's why I think we failed to stop this happening. For that's something I'm bitterly sorry.

Moore-Bick   Thank you very much.

Slide: 'From the evidence of:
LORD PICKLES
Secretary of State for Communities and Local Government May
2010–May 2015
6–7 April 2022'.

6 April 2022.

Moore-Bick   Today we're going to hear evidence from
Lord Pickles. Yes, Mr Millett.

Millett   Lord Pickles, you held the position of Secretary of
State for Communities and Local Government from 12 May
2010 to 11 May 2015. That was the coalition government,
wasn't it?

Pickles   That is correct.

Millett   Now, can we go to paragraph 11 of your statement
on page 3 {CLG00019471/3}. You say there: 'As Secretary of
State, I had overall responsibility for the leadership and
strategic direction of the Department. I was required to have
– and did have – an overview of the work being done by the
Department.'

At the time did anybody bring to your attention any issues or
work being done in relation to fire safety?

Pickles   No.

Millett   Did you at any time become familiar with the
specific functional requirement in the Building Regulations
relating to fire safety?

Pickles   No.

Millett   *No.* Were you ever aware of the particular dangers
posed in high-rise buildings by the use of combustible
materials in the external wall build-up?

Pickles   No, and when I did become aware after I was
Secretary of State, I found that really shocking.

Millett   And when was that?

Pickles   This would be I suppose, what, 2017, 2018.

Millett   So after Grenfell?

Pickles   Oh, yeah, absolutely. There wasn't a single question about cladding, in the whole of the five years that I was Secretary of State, from Parliament, which is generally a pretty good indication if there is a problem.

Millett   Right.

Pickles   Nobody spoke to me about cladding.

Millett   Were you aware that your own officials had looked into the question whether a fire such as happened in Dubai in 2015, high-rise buildings clad in ACM panels with a polyethylene core, could happen here in England and Wales, and had satisfied themselves, without guarantees, of course, that it could not?

Pickles   No.

Millett   Were you absolutely clear that it was clear to all the officials that Approved Document B, which is all about life safety were clearly exempt from the Red Tape [deregulation] Challenge?

Pickles   I expect the process of that kind of message to be taken care of by officials. These are people that I never met.

It's not that I was too snooty or I didn't want to meet them, but at my level, these are people that I would not normally meet.

Millett   Are you aware of any policy statement, strategy document which you knew was in the hands of your top officials which exempted fire safety in the Building Regulations from the Red Tape Challenge or the other deregulatory agendas?

Pickles   I have no memory of it.

Millett   Does it surprise you that no exemptions for the life safety parts of the Building Regulations were ever considered within the Department?

Pickles   I don't find it suprising, I find it astounding.

Millett   Right. Were there in fact any positive policies in place at the time to ensure that Departments such as yours discharged their obligations to protect life, including under Article 2 [of European Convention on Human Rights]?

Pickles   I cannot recall any occasion where I was asked to make that kind of judgement.

Millett   Did you at any time meet Brian Martin or any other officials or junior ministers with knowledge of the approved [building regulations] documents?

Pickles   I don't believe I've ever met Mr Martin.

Millett   Right.

Pickles   And nor would I, at my level.

Millett   Let's go to your statement, please, page 14 {CLG00019471/14}, paragraph 48. You say there: 'I was keen to ensure that all of the Coroner's recommendations [after the Lakanal House fire in Camberwell, south London, in 2009] were properly addressed. I had been a councillor in Bradford at the time of the Bradford City stadium fire, and was acutely aware of the horrors of fire, and the need to do everything possible to avert future tragedies.'

Given that, how was the timetable that you sent back to the coroner, which was a timetable which would finish, let it be assumed, March 2017, for the sake of argument, consistent with working as fast as possible to avert future tragedies?

Pickles   It was clear from the advice that I received from officials that it wasn't possible to do it quicker and to do a thorough job.

Millett   So does it come to this, Lord Pickles, that you were given to believe that only a full review of Approved Document B could address the [Lakanal House] coroner's recommendations and that had to take until 2016/2017 because of the complexities involved?

Pickles   I think that's close to what was said. It was complex and very difficult. But the undertakings that I gave to the coroner weren't followed with the speed and the precision that I would have hoped.

7 April 2022.

Millett   On the subject of deregulation.

Pickles   Okay.

Millett   Now, can we start with {HOM00018307}, please. Now, this is a letter from the then Prime Minister, Mr David Cameron –

Pickles   Yes.

Millett   – dated 6 April 2011, and it starts: 'Dear Colleagues.' The [second] paragraph is about tackling regulation 'with vigour both to free businesses to compete and to create jobs, and to give people greater freedom and personal responsibility. Of course we need proper standards, for example in areas like fire safety and food safety.'

And it goes on, touching on issues about ice cream van jingles and bed prices. 'Be in no doubt: all those unnecessary rules that place ridiculous burdens on our businesses and on society – they must go, once and for all.'

Pickles   This is not an edict that you would get from say, a medieval monarch, this is an encouragement.

Millett   Let's look perhaps at page 3 {HOM00018307/3}.

Pickles   Okay.

Millett   'I look forward to welcoming rapid progress on this agenda in the months ahead. Make no mistake: this is essential work. It will help us build a more dynamic economy, and it will help to build a stronger society. Above all, it will help rebuild in our country the sense of responsibility that is so vital – and which has been so undermined by years of over-regulation.

'I am copying this letter to all Government Ministers . . . to make tackling unnecessary regulation a key priority for the whole of Government.'

In the light of those two paragraphs, how could you not take what the Prime Minister was saying seriously?

Pickles   I don't think at any time during the discussions that we've had and the various ways in which you've essentially asked the same question six or seven times, I have said anything that suggests I didn't take it seriously.

I fully appreciate, sir, this is not a criticism, you are not familiar with the way government works. I think you're giving an importance to this document that if we were . . . if the Prime Minister, the former Prime Minister, were giving evidence, even he would be surprised . . . But, I mean, unless you're about to play a conference speech from the Prime Minister where he would say something like that – but it has the same status as that kind of thing. I'm genuinely sorry that you don't get it.

Millett   Let's go to {CLG10004826}, please.

Pickles   Okay.

Millett   This is an email dated 24 June 2011, so about two and a half months after the letter that we've just seen from the Prime Minister, and it's from Jane Houghton in your Department. You may not know who she is. Do you know who she is?

Pickles   I think I vaguely do.

Millett   Right. Who was she? Can you help us?

Pickles   Not really. I think – I don't know her official title, but I do vaguely remember meeting someone called Jane.

Millett   It reads as follows: 'PICKLES INTRODUCES NEW RED TAPE TEST FOR DEPARTMENT. All future policy at DCLG will be subject to new bureaucracy busting tests as Ministers introduce new red tape challenge to policies. CUTTING DOWN RED TAPE REGULATION FOR THE CONSTRUCTION INDUSTRY.'

Now, would you agree that this shows quite some zeal on your part not only for the deregulatory agenda in general, but to place the Building Regulations firmly within it?

Pickles   Well, I congratulate you, you've managed to find a document with even less status than the Prime Minister's 'Dear colleague' letter. Jane was a middle-ranking press officer.

Millett   Was it the case, as a matter of fact, that your Department was conducting a 2013 Building Regulations review of building standards and the building control system, both to ensure fitness for purpose and quote 'to identify opportunities to deregulate where possible'? Close quote. Was that a fact?

Pickles   But there is nothing to mine here. There is nothing in this document. It was not approved by me, and her reference to any Building Regulations, this would be about something she's been told.

But by all means, sir, feel free to ask me as many questions as like, but could I respectfully remind you that you did promise that we would be away this morning, and I have changed my schedules to fit this in. I do have an extremely busy day meeting people, but this is more important than anything. But I would urge you to use your time wisely.

Millett   Right. May I please have an answer to my question? It's a question of –

Pickles   I have answered it. I've answered it to the point of exhaustion. This document has no status. The information that she has is second-hand. But I'm not going to answer a question that suggests for one moment that this document represents government policy or represents anything other than press releases.

Moore-Bick   Lord Pickles, let me see if I can –

Pickles   I'm sorry, sir.

Moore-Bick   No, no –

Pickles   I don't want to appear rude.

Moore-Bick   I wasn't going to suggest that you were. All I was going to suggest – I mean, I can understand your obvious frustration at being asked so many questions about a document which you think, if I've understood you correctly, amounts to little more than froth, the press office looking for something to say.

But I think what Mr Millett would like a simple answer to is whether, as far as you can recall at this time, the Department was conducting a review of Building Regulations to see whether there were opportunities for deregulation. Now, you may or not remember, but if you do, can you tell us.

Pickles   I don't remember. Could I just ask one point. I am at your disposal. I will be here as long as you are. But I've got a number of international guests coming in to see me. If you think I'm going to go into the afternoon session, I would like to start cancelling.

Moore-Bick   Yes, all right.

Pickles   Should I start cancelling?

Moore-Bick   Well, I can't tell you that, because only Mr Millett knows how long he thinks he might take with his questions, but what I shall do is to ask him, and if he thinks that we may need you in the afternoon, then I'll ask him to let your counsel and solicitors know that, and they are able to tell you or at least to discuss with you whether you need to start cancelling.

Pickles   Yes. I would like as much as possible, because people have literally travelled from other countries to talk to me, so I need to . . .

Moore-Bick   Yes. Well, I'll ask Mr Millett to let your lawyers know before the end of the break how he sees things going. Is that all right?

Pickles   That's extraordinarily kind.

Moore-Bick   Thank you very much.

Pickles   Okay.

Moore-Bick   Would you go with the usher, then, please.

Pause.

Thank you very much.

Short adjournment.

Moore-Bick   All right, Lord Pickles?

Pickles   Sir, could I just – I'd like to apologise if in any way I seemed discourteous. As soon as I left the room, I took the decision to cancel everything. This is more important than anything I'm doing, and I apologise particularly to you, Mr Millett, if in any way I seemed as though I was being discourteous. I fully understand that you're doing a proper job.

Millett   Thank you, Mr Pickles. Could it be the case that you are completely mistaken and that, in fact, no part of the Building Regulations, including the Approved Document B, was at any time exempted from the Red Tape Challenge or the one-in, one-out or one-in, two-out policies?

Pickles   I would have expected, if there was a problem where safety was being compromised, given that we have gone through this entire process, to have been informed by the relevant director or, more particularly, the Permanent Secretary.

Millett   Are you able to account for how it comes about that you didn't know at the time that your officials working in your Department on the Building Regulations and specifically part B [on fire safety] thought they were subject to these de-regulatory policies when it's your evidence that they weren't?

Pickles   I find it utterly inexplicable. I am genuinely amazed.

Millett   Well, you say you find it utterly inexplicable. Let me put an explanation before you, and see what you make of it.

Pickles   Okay.

Millett   One explanation, Lord Pickles, is that you were spectacularly out of touch with what was happening in your Department.

Pickles   I think that would be uncharacteristically unjust of you to say that, because I think you need to bear an understanding that this is an enormous Department, and that I am utterly reliant on receiving good intelligence from my Permanent Secretary and directors to have informed me of where there were problems in Departments where people were not coping.

Millett   Do you take responsibility, ultimate responsibility –

Pickles   Yes, yes, of course. Ultimately, everything is done in my name, and ultimately, the nature is you can't – if you've got full responsibility, that can't be qualified.

The fact that I didn't know, the fact that I had no indication, the fact that I had no opportunity to correct this does not in any way reduce my responsibility.

Millett   There is, Lord Pickles, of course, another explanation, and let me ask you about that, which is that, in fact, your Department was always subject, as the documents we've looked at together might suggest, to the deregulatory agenda, and you're now seeking to recast that narrative and to underplay what was in truth an enthusiasm by your government for a deregulatory agenda which led to a complete absence of proper checks and balances so far as concerns life safety.

Pickles   Again, I think that would be unkind, and I think –

Millett   Is it true?

Pickles   Forgive me, and again I think it would fly in the evidence that you've received. You saw the enormous pressure we were on with regard to fire regulations. You know that it was clear that we realised there was a problem.

So, no, I think that's an unkind characteristic, and I have to say, you know, without getting terribly emotional, I swore on the bloody Bible – I swore on the Bible. I'm a Christian. I wouldn't come here to make some kind of – you know, to try and just try and remove responsibility. These things are important to me.

Millett   What I'd like to do now is to go to the written opening submissions of the Department, which is now called the Department for Levelling Up, Housing and Communities, which deals with your response to the coroner [at the Lakanal House inquest].

Can you explain why your response to the coroner did not articulate in clear terms that the work the coroner had recommended be done was not considered by you to be safety critical?

Pickles   Because of the advice that I received.

Millett   As Secretary of State, do you accept that it was your ultimate responsibility to ensure that your Department followed through with the response to the Coroner in a timely manner, giving the recommendations the ministerial and departmental priority that they deserved?

Pickles   Of course, it 's got to be my responsibility. Even if I wasn't aware, even if, you know – even if people were continuously telling me, I'm the Secretary of State, so ultimately it's my responsibility. But I have to say, as a matter of fact, there was no indication from anyone that there was a problem.

Millett   Looking back on your time as Secretary of State and looking back over the evidence is there anything you would have done differently?

Pickles   Maybe I should have put in the letter [to the Lakanal House coroner on the need for new and clear fire safety rules] the simple sentence, 'and I accept the coroner's recommendations'. Would that have changed things? Your diligence have made me come to the view: I don't think it would have made any difference whatsoever.

I think there was a kind of mindset that existed in parts of the Department that just simply ignored what was happening, the conditions existed that there were people putting things in, into panels and the like, that were combustible. The idea to me is: how would anybody ever want to do that? How would they ever think it was a good idea? We will see various court cases that will put it together, but ultimately it comes down to the nameless I think it was 96 people who were killed in the Grenfell fire. It's them we should think about when we're arguing the toss. Ultimately, it's that the dead deserve the dignity of being remembered by name, the dead deserve the dignity of a solution, and I'm sure you will come to that.

Slide: 'From the evidence of:
NICK HURD
Minister of State for Policing and the Fire Service June 2017–2019
Minister for Grenfell Victims from 26 June 2017–.'

23 May 2022.

Millett   Mr Hurd, at the time of the Grenfell Tower fire, I think you had just been appointed Minister of State for Policing and the Fire Service.

Hurd   That's correct.

Millett   You had been in post, I think, for something like two days before the fire.

Hurd   I think I was appointed on the Monday evening.

Millett   On 26 June 2017, I think you were appointed Minister for the Victims of the Grenfell Tower Fire; is that right?

Hurd   That's correct.

Millett   What did your role and responsibilities involve?

Hurd   To support the victims unit in trying to give direct assistance where we could to victims – and I know the word 'victims' is sensitive, but I will use it because that was the name of the unit; to try and act as some sort of bridge between the community and central government at a time when it was clearly needed, because the context was one of zero trust and engagement.

Millett   Right. When you stood down [in the general election of] 2019, did anybody take that ministerial post up, on from you?

Hurd   No, the arrangement with the Prime Minister was that I would continue to perform a role on a voluntary basis as an independent adviser to him.

Millett   Now, 15 June [2017 the day after the fire] an extraordinary meeting was convened, yes?

Hurd   Correct.

Millett   And what was the purpose of the meeting?

Hurd   This was one of the worst national disasters to have affected this country in peacetime. Obviously the primary issue was, you know, the local conditions and issues that arise around support for the community affected, but it was a national issue as well in which, you know, MPs were having to cope, having to deal with enquiries from their constituents, who were either very concerned about the event and the response then, or very concerned about their personal safety in the tower blocks they're in. So it was entirely appropriate that, you know, our democracy should not ignore the moment.

Millett   [Let's look at a meeting on the 15th June which] started, at 13.30. You're in the chair. Let's go, please, to page 3 {CAB00002720/3}, then, item 2(a):

'2. Key issues: a) Immediate shelter and medium term rehousing those affected were being placed into hotels for immediate shelter, with 77 from Grenfell Tower.'

Did you have clarity at that meeting about whether those figures of those housed in emergency accommodation related to individuals or households?

Hurd   We were very concerned about the quality of information we had about some very basic things, like how many people were in the tower and how many people actually needed support, and when we come on to [Nicholas] Holgate [the Chief Executive of Kensington and Chelsea's] testimony, that was at the crux of his lack of credibility.

Millett   You had been aware of, from earlier that morning, this problem about numbers and consistency?

Hurd   Yes, our knowledge of how many people were in the tower and how many people needed support was not fit for purpose.

Millett   Let's just leave that document on the screen, and can we then go at the same time, please, to {HOM00046089/21}. This is the bundle of situational reports, and this one is at 9.00 am on 15 June, as you can see; yes?

Hurd   Yes.

Millett   It's sitrep 5. If you go, please, down to page 22 it says:

'Vulnerable people and families have been given accommodation overnight as a priority, including 44 families from the tower.'

Now, that's what you were told earlier in the day, but come the afternoon, the meeting discusses 77 from Grenfell Tower as opposed to 44 families. Did you think those figures were inconsistent?

Hurd   I think that reinforces the point I'm making – we couldn't rely on the numbers being provided.

Millett   Right. Did you leave this meeting feeling reassured that the resources and capacity were in place to support those affected by the fire?

Hurd   The overall and most powerful recollection was the complete collapse in the credibility of Nicholas Holgate when under questioning. That is the overriding impression of this meeting.

Millett   Right. Let's pinpoint it exactly in your first statement. Can we go to that, please, at page 5 {HOM00046080/5}, paragraph 17. You say, about three-quarters of the way down the block of text, that you began to lose faith in [Kensington and Chelsea's] ability to deal with the situation. At what point on the 15th of June did you begin to lose faith in [the council]?

Hurd   This was the first time, effectively, the council was kind of open to questions and [Nicholas Holgate] really wasn't able to answer some questions that anyone might reasonably ask him – expect him – to answer.

Millett   Can you give us a concrete example of a question which he wasn't able to answer which you had been expecting him to be able to answer?

Hurd   It was quite clear that the council weren't on top of the numbers, both in terms of numbers of people in the tower and the broader housing requirement, and I can still see the faces round the room of incredulity.

It was a defining moment, it was the moment when I think the system belatedly recognised that the council were failing and that something needed to change, and I think it's from that moment on that the wheels started to turn.

Millett   What measures were in place to monitor that [the council] had the necessary resources from central government effectively to be able to carry out their responsibilities from the start?

Hurd   My short answer is they were inadequate. I and the rest of the system were getting very frustrated about the lack of our understanding of what was really happening on the ground, and that suggested a major information failure.

Millett   Sticking with paragraph 17 {HOM00046080/5}, in the last sentence there you say: 'Further, I appreciate that, given the scale of the disaster, it is likely that [the council] was quite simply overwhelmed.'

Now, is that a hindsight observation?

Hurd   It was fast becoming the impression at the moment. The picture was emerging very clearly of totally unacceptable co-ordination and support for the community.

There was a kind of ground truth lag. Mr Holgate was trying to maintain a line that the council could cope on its own, and the evidence was beginning to weigh very heavily that they couldn't.

Millett   Just one [last] question, Mr Hurd, and it's this: reflecting on it now, is there anything that you would have done differently?

Hurd   Well, I'm ashamed, you know, of the failure of the system I was part of to provide fellow citizens with the most basic support and comfort that they had every reason to feel totally entitled to in arguably their darkest hour.

I've thought hard about this. I was part of a system that failed to be alive early enough to the probability that the Kensington and Chelsea Council would not be able to cope. Add to that the very clear impression that was forming quickly on the first day that the council was going to struggle to have the moral authority to lead. I think that we collectively should have been quicker to put in place risk monitoring that gave us more direct observation of what was happening on the ground that in turn might have empowered us to be more effective in our challenge of the council.

I have a second reflection. Parts of what upsets me most about the evidence that you have been presented with from bereaved, survivors and residents was the way people were made to feel, and you've had language like this – impersonal, second-class citizens, the specific instances of – totally unacceptable.

And I was concerned then and am still concerned now about the degree to which those involved in the human contact in the emergency response are trauma informed. We are talking about a community in deep trauma and those helping them, or trying to help them, need to be, in my view, better informed about what that actually means, and I don't feel that's been picked up elsewhere, but it's very clear to me.

I have just one closing comment with your permission, Chair.

Moore-Bick   Of course.

Hurd   The road to recovery and what some people call a
new normal is still work in progress and continues to be very
difficult for many people.

One observation I make is: where any progress has been
made is where the state has realised that it needed to think
and act differently, the critical distinction between doing
things with people rather than doing things to people.

To make that work, you need people to work with, you
know, individuals, families, committees, representative
groups who took in many ways a very brave decision to
engage with us despite everything that was going on in their
lives, despite every reason not to trust the state, took a
decision that they wanted to work with us to try and help us
make better decisions on behalf of their representatives or
their neighbours, and I know many people would just want
to register our thanks and gratitude for that. It's an
extraordinary community that deserved a lot better. Thank
you.

Moore-Bick   Thank you.

Slide: 'Continuation of the hearing of the evidence of:
HISAM CHOUCAIR
who lost six members of his family in the fire'.

13 April 2022.

Millett   Mr Choucair, I have come pretty much to the end
of my questions. I just have one more for you and that is
whether after taking you back this morning through the
experiences of that time is there anything you would like
to add?

Pause.

Choucair   Erm . . . Where do you begin? Erm . . . There
would be many things I would like to add, or hope for this
Inquiry to take into consideration. Erm . . . Atrocity is one of
them, of the reasons why what happened. To maybe look

into the issue of racism that, through evidence, has – the lack of urgency, because of people's ethnic background and culture, which I don't believe this Inquiry has touched to a certain extent on, that they should.

I don't think I could sum up what everyone had to go through on that day, but it was the most painful experience in my life, that until today won't go, no matter how much counselling or support I receive, myself or my family, and . . . Erm . . .

I'm sorry, but I'm overwhelmed by your question, that I can't really respond in the manner that I feel I should.

Millett   That's all right.

Slide: 'Ten-Minute Break'.

Choucair   First of all, I'd like to thank the Inquiry for giving me the opportunity to, at my pace, answer your questions and to elaborate on what happened on the night and the aftermath. The other thing I wish to say is that I hope that through your recommendations, sir, you will make sure that this doesn't happen again, and I hope that your recommendations will be fulfilled, and you will do something in your power to make sure that they are fulfilled.

The second thing I wish to say is: London has problems. London requires, in my opinion, a resilience centre, somewhere where, in the event of a tragedy or disaster, one wouldn't have to go to numerous places; an all-in-one building, if you wish, where all these resources and help could be given.

And combustible materials, well, need I say more about that? In my opinion, that's obvious what needs to be done there: the removal of combustible materials and the end to combustible materials.

And, erm, lessons need to be learnt, whether they may be from recruitment, training. I mean, if you look at the 7/7 bombs [in 2005], which I was there on the scene, having worked for Transport for London, that happened in numerous places, and we were more in control of that situation, despite the tragedy that happened, than what happened at Grenfell, which was in one place.

So I hope that lessons will be learnt, and you will make sure, through your recommendations, and through listening to the bereaved, survivors and whoever else, that this doesn't happen ever again. And thank you for your time.

Millett   Thank you very much.

Moore-Bick   Thank you.

Blackout.

Slide: Victim's names.

End of Play.

Postscript

Richard Norton-Taylor and Nicolas Kent

Sir Martin Moore-Bick, a former senior judge, is expected later this year (2023) to publish his long-awaited report on the Grenfell Tower fire which killed 72 people, the deadliest residential fire since the Blitz. His report will be meticulous. It will also be devastating.

The consequences of the fire, and the shocking testimony from families of the victims, executives from the companies involved in the refurbishment of Grenfell Tower, from firefighters, from officials in the Royal Borough of Kensington and Chelsea and central government, and from ministers, continues to resonate far beyond the bereaved West London community so traumatised by the disaster.

Our new play will draw fresh attention to important evidence about one of the most scandalous events in recent British history.

In a powerful, withering, final speech at the end of 400 days of testimony (see below) Richard Millett KC, chief counsel to the Inquiry, concluded: 'Each and every one of the deaths that occurred in Grenfell Tower, on the 14 June 2017 was avoidable.'

In other closing speeches, the Inquiry heard Jason Beer KC, the barrister representing the Department for Levelling Up, Housing and Communities, which is now responsible for housing, apologised for its failure to ensure effective oversight of residential buildings. The inquiry heard that safety tests in 2001 demonstrated the extreme flammability of the cladding used years later to refurbish the Grenfell Tower and ministers and officials failed to implement recommendations by the coroner investigating a fatal fire at Lakanal House, a tower block in South London, in 2009.

The government failed to implement any of the major recommendations made by the Inquiry after its first phase in

2019, including providing communal fire alarms in high-rise buildings, and evacuation plans for the disabled. The Home Office in May 2022 said this would not be 'proportionate'. At the beginning of 2023, it was still unclear who would pay the estimated £15 billion cost of making high-rise residential buildings safe, uncertainty leaving hundreds of thousands of tenants and leaseholders with the prospect of continuing to live in potentially dangerous homes and unsellable properties.

Lawyers for the Grenfell Tower families were blunt. The Inquiry had uncovered a 'host of public sector services in decline, including the privatisation of the management of local authority housing, and the degraded function of its building control' that was 'accelerated as part of austerity politics following the global financial crash', Danny Friedman KC representing a group of the bereaved, survivors, and residents, told the Inquiry. He called the fire 'a human rights disaster, a systematic failure of state and private actors to protect the life, security and dignity of people.'

The fire disproportionately killed people with disabilities, those of a migrant background, and those living in social housing,' he noted, and criticised the government for rejecting the Inquiry's recommendations for evacuation plans for residents with disabilities and the failure to recognise the needs of some of the most vulnerable in society.

Stephanie Barwise KC, also representing families, referred to a 'rogues' gallery' including Arconic, the US-owned company that made the highly combustible cladding panels responsible for the fire spreading so quickly, the architect Studio E, and the fire engineer Exova.

She referred to the Inquiry's evidence that Laura Johnson, Kensington and Chelsea borough's housing director, rejected an annual inspection programme of door closers on grounds of cost despite requests from the London Fire

Brigade. Door closers were missing on the night of the fire, encouraging the spread of the fire and smoke. 'This conscious cost-benefit analysis with human life as the cost was not a legitimate way for a local authority to behave,' Barwise said.

Celotex, which made most of the combustible insulation on the Tower, and Kingspan, which also provided insulation material, 'were fraudulent in their sales tactics and in their dealings with those who were charged with testing and certifying the products,' said Adrian Williamson KC. Studio E, Harley, the facade contractor, and Exova were described by Michael Mansfield KC as being 'grossly negligent'.

Greed was a key motivator in the tower's refurbishment and private companies had shown 'a callous indifference to anything – morality, honesty, life safety – that was not related to the bottom line of the business,' said Imran Khan (now a KC), who represented other families. 'Institutional racism infected every aspect of the disaster,' he said, chiding the Inquiry panel for not considering whether race and the social background of the Grenfell Tower residents played a part in the disaster. He said that was a failure, what he called a 'missed opportunity to change the lives of millions of people of colour' in Britain.

The companies involved attempted to deny responsibility for the 72 deaths. Arconic said that if others involved in the tower's refurbishment had properly read a safety certificate for its cladding panels which said they were combustible, very likely no one would have died. Stephen Hockman KC, lawyer for the large US-owned corporation, said other companies' blaming Arconic was a 'very convenient way of avoiding their own responsibility'. It was 'unjust' and 'profoundly disappointing' to claim Arconic had misled the market, he claimed, suggesting that its cladding produces less heat than the contents of the flats in Grenfell Tower. Expert witnesses established that 'at least half of the heat loading occurred as a result of the combustion of the apartment contents rather than the combustion of the components of the cladding system,' he told the Inquiry.

Jonathan Laidlaw KC, for Harley Facades, conceded there had been 'failings' and 'omissions'. But he added that the government had failed to intervene to stop Arconic's cladding when tests before the fire showed the material burned like an 'inferno'.

Geraint Webb KC, who represented Kingspan, maker of some of the insulation material used in the tower, told the closing stages of the Inquiry: 'A significant share of the responsibility for the tragedy of Grenfell Tower rests with Arconic as a manufacturer of the polyethylene ACM material.'

In his closing speech addressing the Inquiry chair, Millett said every one of the risks which led to the fire 'were well known by many and ought to have been known by all who had any part to play. As a result, you will be able to conclude with confidence that each and every one of the deaths that occurred in Grenfell Tower on 14 June 2017 was avoidable'.

Millett continued: 'The reasons were many, complex and in many cases inextricably interlinked . . . It is open to you on the evidence to conclude that there was a long run-up of incompetence and poor practices in the construction industry and the fire engineering and architects' profession; weak and incompetent building control; cynical and possibly even dishonest practices in the cladding and insulation materials manufacturing sector; incompetence, weakness and malpractice by those responsible for testing and certifying those materials; the failure of central government to act, despite known risks; failures of competence, training and oversight within the TMO [Kensington and Chelsea's Tenant and Management Organisation], and over it by RBKC [the Royal Borough of Kensington and Chelsea]; a failure by the LFB [London Fire Brigade] to learn the lessons of Lakanal, and other fires, and to train its operational staff to collect, understand and to act on the risks presented by modern construction methods and materials; risks well known to some, but not all, within that institution.'

'Behind all of these discrete factors,' said Millett, 'there lay complex, opaque and piecemeal legislation, and an over-reliance by law and policymakers on guidance, some of which – including the statutory guidance – was ambiguous, dangerously out of date, and much of which was created by non-governmental bodies and influenced by commercial interests.'

Millett spoke of 'policies pursued by successive governments; a fundamental failure to understand and to assess fire risk in high-rise blocks; and a concomitant failure to pay due respect to the idea of home as a physical aspect of human privacy, agency, safety and dignity.' He added: 'If everything that has been said is correct, then nobody was to blame for the Grenfell Tower fire. Can that really be right?'

He then said: 'When I opened this Inquiry as counsel . . . I told you that all the indications were to be that some, at least, of the core participants would indulge in what I termed a "merry-go-round of buck-passing"'. Millett said he had hoped his task and that of the chair of the Inquiry would be made easier by candid admission of blame. Some core participants, principally public bodies, had made what he called 'carefully expressly admissions of specific fault'.

He went on: 'My metaphor may now have become rather worn but for many even now the merry-go-round turns still, the notes of its melody clearly audible . . . Expressions of regret for the victims of the fire have been as common, to the point of trite, as admissions of responsibility have been rare. A tragedy of these dimensions ought to have provoked a strong sense of public responsibility. Instead, many – not all, many – core participants appear simply to have used the Inquiry as an opportunity to position themselves for any legal proceedings which might or might not follow in order to minimise their own exposure to legal liability'.

Quite apart from the lack of respect that that stance showed to the victims and their families, it made the Chairman of the Inquiry Sir Martin Moore-Bick's task all the harder. A public inquiry was 'not the place for cleverness, but for candour', said Millett.

After Millett spoke, Grenfell United, the families' group, said the closure of the Inquiry was a reminder 'that we continue to live our lives knowing the evidence has been uncovered. And yet, there's no change. No accountability. No charges'.

It added: 'We now have to put our faith into a justice system that protects the powerful – a system that prevents justice. While this system exists, we face the same unachievable battle as the many before us. From Aberfan, to Hillsborough, justice has been denied, and Grenfell is no different.'

The Royal Borough of Kensington and Chelsea saved just £293,368 by the disastrous decision to switch from zinc cladding to combustible plastic-filled aluminium panels. Kensington and Chelsea borough spent more than £400 million on its response to the fire. The Inquiry, which disclosed more than 320,000 documents, has cost about £150 million, much of it on legal bills alone. The total legal bill is much higher. The cladding manufacturer, Arconic, for example, has spent over £3 million every three months on lawyers. The Metropolitan Police will wait for the full Inquiry to report before handing evidence to the Crown Prosecution Service which will decide whether criminal charges will be brought. Potential crimes include corporate manslaughter, gross negligence manslaughter, fraud and health and safety offences. A separate high court civil litigation is underway with more than 1,100 members of the Grenfell family community taking action against emergency responders, the Royal Borough of Kensington and Chelsea council, and Arconic, the cladding manufacturer. Lord Neuberger, a former supreme court president, is acting as a mediator. The actions could result in multi-million-pound compensation and admissions of responsibility.

There are plans to turn the remains of Grenfell Tower, or more probably its site, into a permanent memorial. A commission has recently visited a memorial to the Manchester Arena bombing, which took place three months before the Grenfell disaster. The community is being consulted in about what form a memorial should take, whether it should be a place for children's activities, or simply a space for the bereaved to come together.

(In an email to the Inquiry after he gave evidence, Lord Pickles apologised for referring to 96 people he suggested had died in the fire. That was the number of people who died in the 1989 Hillsborough football stadium disaster.)

THE 72 VICTIMS

Marco Gottardi, Gloria Trevisan, Raymond Bernard, Fethia Hassan, Hania Hassan, Rania Ibrahim, Hesham Rahman, Mohamed Neda, Fathia Elsanosi, Abufars Ibrahim, Isra Ibrahim, Zainab Choucair, Mierna Choucair, Fatima Choucair, Bassem Choucair, Nadia Choucair, Sirria Choucair, Firdaws Hashim, Yaqub Hashim, Yahya Hashim, Hashim Kedir, Nura Jemal, Anthony Disson, Mariem Elgwahry, Eslah Elgwahry, Ligaya Moore, Mehdi El-Wahabi, Nur Huda El-Wahabi, Yasin El-Wahabi, Faouzia El-Wahabi, Abdulaziz l-Wahabi, May Ajaoi Augustus Mendy, Khadija Saye, Malak Belkadi, Leena Belkadi, Omar Belkadi, Farah Hamdan, Jessica Urbano Ramirez, Gary Maunders, Deborah Lamprell, Ernie Vital, Marjorie Vital, Mohamednur Tuccu, Amaya Tuccu-Ahmedin, Amal Ahmedin, Amna Mahmud Iris, Fatemeh Afrasiabi, Sakineh Afrasiabi, Isaac Paulos, Hamid Kani, Biruk Haftom, Berkti Haftom, Vincent Chiejina, Mohammed Hanif, Mohammed Hamid, Husna Begum, Rabeya Begum, Kamru Miah, Khadija Khaloufi, Joseph Daniels, Sheila, Steven Power, Denis Murphy, Mohammed Al-Haj Ali, Jeremiah Deen, Zainab Deen, Abdeslam Sebbar, Ali Yawar Jafari, Victoria King, Alexandra Atala, Logan Gomes, Maria Del Pilar Burton.